SPANISH POINTERS

•

Jackie Todd

TRAFFORD
PUBLISHING™

• Canada • UK • Ireland • USA •

Note for Librarians: a cataloguing record for this book that includes Dewey Decimal Classification and US Library of Congress numbers is available from the Library and Archives of Canada. The complete cataloguing record can be obtained from their online database at:
www.collectionscanada.ca/amicus/index-e.html
ISBN 1-4120-6490-2
Printed in Victoria, BC, Canada

Printed on paper with minimum 30% recycled fibre. Trafford's print shop runs on "green energy" from solar, wind and other environmentally-friendly power sources.

Offices in Canada, USA, Ireland and UK
This book was published *on-demand* in cooperation with Trafford Publishing. On-demand publishing is a unique process and service of making a book available for retail sale to the public taking advantage of on-demand manufacturing and Internet marketing. On-demand publishing includes promotions, retail sales, manufacturing, order fulfilment, accounting and collecting royalties on behalf of the author.

Book sales for North America and international:
Trafford Publishing, 6E–2333 Government St.,
Victoria, BC v8t 4p4 CANADA
phone 250 383 6864 (toll-free 1 888 232 4444)
fax 250 383 6804; email to orders@trafford.com
Book sales in Europe:
Trafford Publishing (uk) Ltd., Enterprise House, Wistaston Road Business Centre,
Wistaston Road, Crewe, Cheshire cw2 7rp UNITED KINGDOM
phone 01270 251 396 (local rate 0845 230 9601)
facsimile 01270 254 983; orders.uk@trafford.com
Order online at:
trafford.com/05-1401

10 9 8 7 6 5 4 3

FOR STEPHEN

•

Thank you.
Gilda O'Neill for getting me started.
Chet and Gretchen Wolford for helping me through.
Hilary Johnson for finishing me off.

•

Front cover left to right:
Tin Tin, Domingo, Niña and Charly in the window of La Panificadora.

ISLINGTON, LONDON,
EARLY 1990's

———

'We can't have a dog in London, we're out all day, it just wouldn't be fair.'

'I know that.'

'When we live in Spain, OK?'

'Stephen. That will be written on my grave.'

'Please, don't start.'

'I'm not starting. Actually, I don't start, as you put it.' What sort of dog shall we get?'

'A Spanish Pointer of course.'

'And, when we finally, finally move to Spain, we can have a cat too, can't we?'

'Of course.'

'Two. Two of those beautiful Mediterranean tabbies, the ones with the lovely charcoal stripes that match across their front legs and the Cleopatra eyeliner.'

'Yes. When we live in Spain, OK?'

'OK. So it's all decided then, a Spanish Pointer and two Mediterranean tabbies.'

CASA ROSA

———

We bought Casa Rosa as a home for holidays in the late Spring of 1991. Stephen quite rightly calls that trip the most expensive holiday he has ever had. Earlier that year, against stiff competition, we had won the contract to design the new offices for The Economist. I clearly remember sitting in the back of a black cab, driving away from Duke Street, pissed off that I didn't have time to enjoy Selfridges, delighted to know that the job was ours, but less than impressed that it was going to be a very fast track project. It would certainly mean that we would not be having a holiday that summer

A couple of weeks later, The Economist lost the building they wanted. Knowing that there was going to be a pause, we grabbed at the chance of a quick break. Thelma, Stephen's mum, had for many years owned a charming little house in Capistrano, one of the first developments in the hills just above Nerja, on

the Eastern Costa del Sol. We were on the first plane
to Malaga the following morning.

'We love Spain, we really should think about getting
a place out here for ourselves.'

Stephen has a habit of coming out with these casual
one-liners that sometimes change our lives. This, although I didn't spot it at the time, was one of them.

It did make sense as we had cancelled numerous
holidays, often at short notice and great expense to
bow to the demands of our clients. A place of our
own, in an area that we loved, would give us much
more freedom. During that week, whilst looking at
many houses, we found our first Antonio. Antonio the
Estate Agent, a completely different animal from the
English breed. Like all in his trade he obviously wanted to sell us a house, but he genuinely came across as
caring that we were going to be happy with our pur-
chase and worked hard to that end. He enquired about
our dream, our lifestyle, he collected us in his car, he
bought us lunch in tiny hidden tapas bars where we
were greeted as family and took us to every conceivable type of house. We saw beautiful places in the middle of nowhere, or so it seemed to me, at least thirty
minutes along crumbling dirt tracks totally unpassable
in the winter rains and an hour's drive to buy bread
or milk. We looked at, and were sorely tempted by, a
charming house that was accessed by the river bed of
the Rio Seco and lovingly restored by the owner, Jesus.
He had used the traditional building methods, antique
wall tiles, terracotta floors and old olive wood beams,

to bring the house back to its prime in the days when his grandparents had lived there. The only thing that really put us off was the uncertainty about where the proposed future motorway would pass. Thank goodness that it did, because the following winter the river bed of Rio Seco (Seco—Dry) looked more like the Manchester Ship Canal and the motorway now runs past the bottom of his orchard.

We viewed lofty penthouse apartments on the concrete coast with jaccuzis on their enormous terraces and gold taps in every bathroom. Tourist ghettos; terraced houses that looked like whitewashed Coronation Streets blessed with sunshine and perma-tanned, peroxide Bet Lynches behind every Black Horse, your-local-away-from-home type bar. We toured estates of newly built villas complete with marble floors and aluminium double glazing, surrounded by ornate white railings topped by bronzed eagles. They resembled wedding cakes and their private pools were overlooked on every side. No. Antonio even took us to Torrox Costa, a mere fifteen minute drive from Nerja and holiday home to half of Germany. There, they don't give their high rise flats names, with typical Germanic efficiency they simply use numbers. Just imagine inviting friends to visit - 'You must come and see our new place, number one hundred and eighty four in block seventeen.'

That week we bought Casa Rosa. We had actually driven past it on our first day out with Antonio. I had noticed the For Sale sign and said that it looked interesting. This he had ignored totally. With hindsight I think that he toured us around the area for a few days waiting to do a deal with the agent who had it on his books, because eventually he casually mentioned the place we had passed on day one. As I had expressed interest, he said, he had arranged for us to see it.

It was beautiful. Part of an old mill complex, dating back to Moorish times. Nine tall steps led up to the heavy stable door, a door that we were soon to learn had a life of its own, swelling with the winter rains and withering in the blast of summer's sun. This door with attitude led straight into the kitchen, a rustic room with sloping beamed ceilings and a thick slab of scarred olive wood, worn smooth over the years, which served as the breakfast bar. The owners proudly showed off the gleaming stainless steel kitchen sink, pointing out that, at great expense, they had only recently replaced the old stone one and its original brass taps. Even this couldn't put me off. The walls were two feet thick, their angles softened by probably thousands of coats of cal, the local limewash. The wooden

floors, very unusual for this area, still showed the well worn paths of the mill workers, despite many layers of linseed oil and varnish. No two rooms were on the same level, there were two steps up to the bedroom off the kitchen, then one step down to the little bathroom on the ground floor.

If there were ever a 'Loo With A View' competition, then I would enter the upstairs bathroom of Casa Rosa. From this elevated throne the mountains soar and the sea twinkles in the distance. Outside there was a secret walled garden, a wisteria and vine-covered terrace threaded with winter jasmine and a jacaranda tree. For me, it was the icing on the cake. It had only two bedrooms. We were looking for three. There was no pool. We would have liked one. In fact Casa Rosa was so far from the brief that we had given Antonio that both he and Stephen stared open mouthed, then put their heads in their hands when I declared that this was it. It was perfect, ideal, just what we were looking for. My explanation that 'it just felt right' went completely over their heads.

Casa Rosa, in the tiny hamlet of La Molineta, is situated just below one of Andalucia's famous pueblos blancos, the stunningly beautiful white mountain village of Frigiliana. Only twenty minutes drive from the coast but a hundred years distant in lifestyle. This was my idea of Spain.

The water that used to power the mills still ran through the gardens, trickling over smooth worn stone, cooling and soothing the senses. Called the acequia, these waterways were built by the Moors in the tenth and eleventh centuries to bring the mountain water, via this network of tiny canals, to irrigate these valleys. An impressive feat of engineering even by today's standards. It was operated and controlled by a series of sluice gates, normally about three feet square sheets of rough metal that were padlocked in place to direct the water flow. The 'acequia man' held the keys to these locks and would spend all of his days, and often parts of his nights as well, going up and down the valley opening and closing the locks, altering the flow depending upon who was entitled to how much water and when.

The value of a campo property has a direct correlation to the amount of water that it has been allocated and at what time. In summer, even if your water allocation is generous, if it is at midday it will evaporate rapidly and barely touch the thirsty dusty soil. One hour of water in the early morning or late in the evening is worth more than three hours mid-afternoon.

These small, irrigated orchards that depend on the acequia water are mainly used for growing avocados, mangos, custard apples and nisperos. The best English—Spanish dictionary we have tells me that nisperos are the fruit of the medlar tree, which means nothing to me. They look and taste like small sweet apricots, are harvested in May, and are said to be kind to the stomach and aid digestion. Until moving here I had never seen any of these fruits growing. A custard apple, called a chirimoya, is a large, rather ugly gnarled-looking fruit that grows on tall strong trees. If you think you might like pureed apple mixed with cold custard, then this is for you. Cut the top off as you would a soft boiled egg, and eat it with a spoon.

One of these water control points was almost directly under our bedroom window and we soon grew accustomed to our six a.m. alarm call that echoed down the valley 'tienes agua?—do you have water?' It was a regular part of life and funnily enough it became one of the many joys of our holidays. To be woken in such a different way from the usual screeching alarm clock, to note the fact that it was six a.m. and the sun was rising. That we didn't have to hit Upper Street or the agression of the Formula One track of the M4, and then to turn over and sleep again, for as long as we wanted, was pure luxury.

Casa Rosa became our perfect bolt hole from a hectic London life. We used it at every opportunity. In the year before moving here we made ten visits, sometimes for little more than forty-eight hours at a time.

We were then and still are Hispanophiles. Like every country, Spain has its faults of course, but here we usually have to search to find them, then we quickly excuse and forgive them.

My first real experience of Spain, or rather my first real experience of real Spain, had been several years before we bought Casa Rosa when Stephen brought me here as a surprise birthday treat in early March. The weather was a bonus, having left London in a blizzard; the sun was strong and I got a genuine red nose on Red Nose Day. But it was discovering the trio of romantic Moorish cities, Cordoba, Granada and Sevilla, with their stunning architecture and proud sense of history, the openness and warmth of their people, and the delicious food that made me begin to realise that I had seriously mis-judged this country.

Much, much earlier than that, my life as a stewardess had meant regularly spending an hour or ten on the tarmac at Malaga airport, white gloves and fixed smile in place. The white gloves give you a clue, it was quite a while ago. With this very limited exposure, I had decided Spain held no interest. Passengers on the outbound journey, having been up since at least three in the morning, were, in general, subdued; however, after two weeks of cheap everything, the return flights were often a nightmare. Even the teetotallers appeared out of it; their home-bound flight seemed to mark the grand finale of their well-earned holiday. Valiantly trying to cram stuffed donkeys, sombreros and castanettes into the overhead lockers, clutching bottles of wine depicting their favourite English football teams and singing 'The Birdy Song' they were ready for their last party. Spain was not for me. How wrong could I be?

SOUTHERN ANDALUCIA, 1997

In March of 1997 we realised our dream and finally moved to Spain. Casa Rosa had served us very well as a holiday home for six years, though if we were to live here permanently our needs were going to be different.

Certainly we would need more space and a pool, but that house had a huge piece of our hearts; we loved the area and our neighbours, we were both so loath to leave it all behind.

With incredible luck/fate/fortune, at exactly the time we had been making the decision to leave the UK, not something we took lightly, the Old Bakery—La Panificadora—adjoining Casa Rosa was offered to us in a private sale. It was the first time it had been on the market since the owners had bought the whole hillside of crumbling mills more than thirty-five years before. Ever since buying Casa Rosa, we had been asking Peter and Felicity, the owners of the rest of the hillside, if we could buy just three metres of the adjoining garden to give us enough space for a pool. The answer had always been a polite but very firm NO. They had stumbled upon the mill buildings in the early sixties after a tip-off from Felecitiy's mother, Rose. Their love of La Molineta in the thirty years they had spent restoring the buildings shone, not only in their stories but also in the houses themselves. We felt honoured to be asked to take on another of their houses; they knew that we would treasure it, as indeed we do.

So the opportunity to buy La Panificadora was the tipping of the scales in our decision to move to Spain. It already had the essential pool, and we could then steal the much needed three metres from our own new home to put a pool into Casa Rosa. Holiday homes without pools understandably don't rent well. We could have our cake and eat it, let Casa Rosa earn its keep and therefore not have to sell it and only have to move next door. We had loved 'The Pan' as it was known locally, since first entering it soon after buying Casa Rosa. Four bedrooms, two bathrooms, huge arched living spaces created from the former grain mill and a generous terraced walled garden. It was a most unusual building. Most old houses in the southern part of Andalucia look like a collection of shoe boxes. Rooms were added when needed and when money allowed; large spaces were not necessary, hard to heat in winter, redundant in summer. Our former mill was a rarity.

There was only one drawback, La Panificadora was rented to a holiday company until the end of that October, and we all agreed that the contract had to be honoured. It was ours on paper, we got the rental income, but we had a six-month wait.

Knowing we were finally on our way, busy selling and packing up in London, we had not been to Casa Rosa since the previous Christmas. Only three months, but three months that had brought the wettest weather that part of Spain had seen for more than ten years, and delighted relief to the local farmers following a full five-year drought.

We arrived at Casa Rosa late one Sunday morning in March after a twenty-eight hour drive, almost without a stop, from the ferry port of Caen on the northern French coast. Not a journey to be recommended.

At two a.m., just north of Madrid and exausted after eighteen hours in the car, we agreed that doing the trip in one drag had been over-ambitious. Actually this is not strictly true, I had said from the start that it was too long a drive and had suggested a stopover, which Stephen had dismissed by saying it would be an adventure. So I was full of 'I told you so's' when we decided to stop at the next hotel.

There weren't any.

Eventually we settled for an hour's doze in the car on the forecourt of a petrol station. Easy for me, five foot four can curl up quite comfortably in a Land Rover and my mother had always said I could sleep on a washing line. For Stephen's six foot plus it was more difficult. Waking, we splashed cold water on our faces, scraped the fur off our teeth, drank nerve-rattling café solos and set off again. Half an hour later, just South of Madrid, the road is lined with hotels.

We had sailed from Portsmouth at eleven p.m. on Friday the 21st, a date that for four months had had stars and asterisks around it in my diary. The diary which also had a count down list of the days and 'To Do' lists of epic proportions. Although we had booked a cabin, were tired and should have slept, we were both too excited. This was the first step of our long-planned adventure. We took our brandies to the stern, waved goodbye to our previous lives and toasted our future.

So, stiff, grubby, exhausted, but still elated, we gently coaxed Casa Rosa's old wooden, rain-swollen stable door open enough for us to just squeeze through. Velvet was very much in fashion at the time and, if nothing else, we were fashionable. Everything was covered in a good inch and a half of the stuff, a smelly, furry black mould. It blossomed from the walls, powdered all the beds and linen right down to the underside of the mattresses, had turned the beige sofas black and even grew on our toothbrushes. When we opened the wardrobes every single item of clothing was black stinking velvet. Every light we turned on blew, showering us with glass and mould. The first two weeks were a blur of bleach and big black bin bags.

At the end of each long day, days that felt like hard labour in comparison to our office-bound previous lives, we repaired to Antonio's bar, less than a minute's walk away, for a medicinal brandy. Antonio would fish his penknife out of a pocket and cut us a few slices of crusty bread to accompany the goats cheese stored in olive oil, so strong that your mouth would feel like it had just sucked a lemon and peppery chorizo sausage. Watching the setting sun turn the mountains first pink, then purple and with its promise to return tomorrow, we listened to the goat bells in the distance, watched the mules silhouetted on the horizon carrying their loads home, and soon remembered why we had chosen to move to this perfect place.

ANTONIO AND HIS BAR

Antonio and his bar. Both have been, and in fact still are, pivotal to the informality of our life here. To Antonio, all the cliches apply: he's a loveable rogue, a rough diamond, a tinker with a heart of gold and an eye to a deal. Years ago, before we grew wise to such things, he warned us of the possible dangers the rotting old ox-cart in front of our house could cause. We were actually rather fond of it. Eventually, for a fair price, he agreed to get rid of it—then sold it to our neighbours. Like most of his generation, he has the sort of olive skin that makes a weathered orange look smooth, and the bloodshot, bloodhound eyes that can only be achieved after many years of sun, sex and sangria. At about five foot three he is of average height for the men of his age, carries a bit too much weight around his middle and nearly always wears a hat. Straw for summer, a new one every year or two, then, as the seasons change, an old grey felt fedora that has seen many winters. It is rumoured that he was the local Romeo, especially for the first foreign women who moved here in the sixties. To be fair to him, the twinkle of the jet black eyes can still be there at times, and once he has decided that you are his friend, it is for life and you can do no wrong.

His long-suffering wife, Rosario, was born in La Molineta sixty eight years ago, the only person to have lived all her life there and she never lets anyone forget it. Every morning I would watch from our kitchen window as she brushed the dust from the road in front of the bar onto the edge of her neighbour's land. An hour or so later, every morning, the neighbour's wife, Pilar, would come out and brush it back again. They could each brush into the gutter, but no—and yet they are still firm friends, have been so from childhood, and never speak of such things.

When we arrived that March, Rosario was recovering from a very badly broken ankle. She had fallen whilst picking avocados and, knowing that Antonio would be in the bar all day, she dragged herself up to the roadside; even now she still has a pronounced limp and uses a walking stick. She was staying with her daughter, Maria, in El Morche, a small and rather ugly village on the coast road back towards Malaga. Like many Spanish villages, the industrial and commercial areas are on the main road, but whereas a little exploring will usually uncover pretty squares and churches, El Morche has none, what you see from that road is as good as it gets.

Hobbling on crutches, there was no way Rosario

could negotiate the steep rough track down to her house below the bar. Maria's flat, on the third floor, has only two bedrooms and their son, evicted from his room, was sleeping on the sofa. Maria loves her mother dearly but not when she is in her house twenty-four hours a day and has a moody displaced teenager to placate, and Rosario was missing La Molineta.

We had begun to convert the ground floor of Casa Rosa into a flat with the idea that my mum may move out here some day, or at least for the winters, something she was still blowing hot and cold about at the time. The bedroom and bathroom were finished and our offer that Rosario might like to spend a few days in our basement was greeted with enthusiasm by all concerned, especially Maria, although I suspect that Antonio's smiles were rather forced; he was enjoying his newly discovered freedom. Rosario moved in the next day - and stayed for nine months.

Antonio's bar is about twelve foot square and opens straight onto the road. It has two tiny wooden tables and six mismatched chairs, a speckled mirror that advertises a long-forgotten gin company and many old newspaper pictures of Franco tacked to the nicotine-stained walls. He opens when he gets up and closes when the last person leaves, often at two or three in the morning A few years ago he acquired an old cassette player and delighted in becoming the 'disco' of La Molineta, playing crackling sevillana and cante jondo, the raw flamenco of Andalucia, at full volume. We have always suspected that he has never learnt to read or write but, like many of his age around here, has learnt to hide the fact pretty well. All drinks, in' 97, were one hundred pesetas, water, wine, beer or brandy. He kept a piece of chalk behind the bar and for every drink ordered he would make a mark on the bar top in front of you; at the end of the evening he counted the marks, multiplied by one hundred, and that was your bill.

One evening, about three weeks after our arrival, we stood, still smelling of bleach, in the doorway of his bar watching blue black dark clouds building up ominously behind the mountains. They were reaching the point where it seemed impossible that the sky could support them any longer.

'Is it going to rain, Antonio?'

He grunted, he scratched his stomach, his crotch, then his stubbly chin and was obviously giving the question some quite serious consideration.

'Yes. But not until the end of October.'

That evening Antonio decided that now we were 'aqui para siempre' (here for ever) it was time to introduce us to the local wine of Frigiliana, in this case, his own brew.

Wine—no problem—I often used to share a bottle or two with girlfriends after work and still be able to walk in a straight line. Vino de terreno, however, proved to be entirely different, more like a strong sherry, and I honestly don't remember leaving the bar or getting to bed that night.

DOG? WHAT DOG?

The following morning at about half-past ten the sun was celebrating my discomfort, sneaking through chinks in the bedroom curtains and drilling into my poor bloodshot eyes. There comes an age when recovering from the excesses of the night before gets harder, and I had to face the fact that I had reached it. With totally unnecessary noise and flourish Stephen banged a cup of black coffee on my bedside table.

'The dog's here and it's gorgeous. I think we should keep him.'

'Dog, what dog?'

'The one you said you would take to the animal rescue charity.'

'When?'

'I don't know when.'

'No. WHEN, when did I SAY that I would take a dog to animal rescue?'

'Last night in Antonio's, to the holiday makers who had seen it thrown out of a car, remember?'

'Umm.'

'They have been feeding it for almost a week, but they go home today. They said it would break their hearts and ruin their holiday if they just walked away not knowing what would become of it, remember?'

'Umm.'

Wrapped in a towel, I shuffled downstairs still clutching my coffee. The dog stood in the kitchen looking at me. It gave a small nervous wag of tail, head on one side. Considering that I had gone to bed in full make-up and now resembled Coco the clown, he was obviously a very polite little boy. My first dog. For both of us, it was love at first sight.

Bad hangovers demanding hearty food, we popped the puppy on the back seat and drove up to El Cerro, one of our favourite restaurants at that time. With views to the sea and the backdrop of mountains, mama in the kitchen and the sons and daughter serving. Esperanza's cooking would do the trick.

Volumes have been written about how to get your new dog used to the car. 'Let doggy sit in it for a few days before you ever even think of driving it anywhere.' Then, 'take the car around the block a few times, driving slowly, nothing more.' Sorry, puppy, we need food.

These were the days before this quaint family restaurant displayed a list of do's and don't's as long as your arm, had a menu in English and NO DOGS signs on every surface. Also the days before Judith Chalmers featured it in some travel programme as one of the 'unspoiled jewels' of the area, always the kiss of death. The puppy wandered around happily.

'What's his name?'

'Sorry?'

'The puppy. What's his name?'

The fuschia pink, freckled seven-year old with ginger hair, two earrings, wearing an Arsenal shirt did actually have a point.

'What shall we call him?'

'Patch.'

'No.'

'Dog?'

'Don't be stupid.'

'Remember Gordon at work? He had a dog called Baxter. It's a good name. Baxter.'

'He's not a Baxter.'

'Well he can't be a blackie or a spot or a snowy or something - he's every colour. How about Patchwork? You enjoy sewing.'

At this stage, our brains were not exactly firing on every cylinder. Resorting to the hair of the dog with no name, we ordered a bottle of vino rosado and, after much creative thinking, decided to call him Charlie.

That should have been more than enough for one day, but Stephen, knowing about such things, decided that in the evening we should take Charlie to a vet to 'just have him checked out', whatever that meant. There are three veterinary practices in Nerja, our nearest town. We chose at random and luck was, as usual, with us.

Rafael and Dolores are a husband and wife team whom, although we didn't realise it at the time, were soon to become invaluable. Whilst Stephen toured the town looking for parking, I carried Charlie inside and was shown straight into the consulting room. I explained, in poor Spanish, that he was an abandoned puppy, that we intended to keep him, and that we just wanted to make sure that he didn't have any major health problems. Rafael gave him a thorough examination: eyes, ears, hip joints, thermometer and a blood test. To break the silence –

'At least he seems to have been well fed. He has a very fat little tummy.'

'Parasitos.'

'Como?'

'He is fat because the parasitos. Parasitos. I give injection.'

With that, he used a syringe-type pump to force some white gunge down Charlie'sthroat. It marked the beginning of his pathological hatred of the vet; nowadays if I even drive down the same street, Charlie howls. Spanish dogs have passports, or at least they should, and Rafael proceeded to make one out for Charlie, estimating his age at about six weeks. He flicked back through his desk diary and, without a word, gave him a birth date of the twenty-second of March, the day we had landed in Spain. I just love fate and the tricks it can play. Back in reception, Stephen had arrived, we paid the bill (less than it would cost to treat a goldfish in the UK) and celebrated our new-found pet ownership by buying a smart little red collar with matching lead and a wicker dog basket with, strangely, pictures of cows in a meadow on its quilted cushion.

Having made a rare evening journey into town from our rural retreat, we decided to stay for tapas and watch the world go by. We sat at one of the many pavement cafes. Tapa is Spanish for 'lid' or 'cover', and the tradition of eating a tapa with your drink dates back to the times of travel by coach and horses. Drinks would be brought to the travellers and, to keep the dust and flies out, a little saucer or a piece of bread was put over the glass. Over time, as competition grew between these inns, a slice of tortilla or ham was added for free. Even today, if you know where to go you can still get a free tapa with every drink. In the tourist bars, they charge outrageously. Our Spanish friends wouldn't dream of drinking anything alcoholic without a tapa to accompany it, don't drink on an empty stomach is something that the English preach and the Spanish practise.

I showed Stephen Charlie's passport.

'Look. Charlie is all official now, he has a passport.'

'Charly?'

'Yes, we agreed at luchtime, Charlie.'

'CharlY. Charlie but with a Y.'

'Let me see. Oh. Oh well, OK, I didn't notice, anyway, I'm sure he won't mind, it sounds the same. The vet was very kind, gentle and thorough and he said

Charly has something called papasitos, but that we weren't to worry. He gave him some stuff and said he will be fine.'

'You mean paRasitos; that's worms.'

Right on cue, Charly realised that something volcanic was happening at his rear end. The action of his trying to turn around and investigate this new sensation resulted in an arc of ... well, I am sure you can imagine. We threw a one thousand peseta note on the table as payment and apology, picked him up carefully and ran.

LIFE WITH A DOG

So we had Charly. Not the Spanish Pointer we had so long imagined, not anything that you could really call a breed. Perhaps one day a labrador may have met his great-great-grandmother, whose daughter then may have had a passing fling with a German Shepherd, but that's about as close as we can guess. With all the colours of a herd of goats and sad, almost transparent, pale hazel green eyes, Charly was born looking old and worried. The only really remarkable thing about him at this stage was his incredibly pink nose. Our French neighbour, Roger, has always called him Truffe Plastique because his nose really does look just like one of the pink plastic ones we used to stick onto potato men when we were kids.

The following day Stephen left before dawn. He had an on-going project and the client refused to deal with anyone but him, so for our first six months in Spain he commuted between Malaga and London, spending four working days, three nights, every other week in London. He hated going, but in a classic case of leaving full-time employment one day and coming back as a consultant the next, it was just too lucrative to turn away.

That morning the builders arrived. Both dogs and Spanish builders were new to me. The team of four started at eight, by which time most of them had had at least two very strong café solos and one, maybe two brandies or annis to 'help their digestion.' The project was a simple one, certainly compared to what we have done since. We wanted to remove the window in the dining room and replace it with glass panelled doors that would lead straight onto the terrace. Well, the coffee, the brandy or, perhaps just the basic Spanish machismo, certainly worked. Within five minutes the window and the wall below it were gone, replaced by a gaping hole and a pile of rubble. Then it started to rain. Not rain as we knew it from England, just a drizzle really but, with much sucking of rotting teeth and shaking of heads, they packed up and left. I chased after Bigote, another Antonio, no more than five feet tall and nicknamed for his impressive big black 'bigote', his moustache.

'Antonio. What's happening?'

'It's raining.'

'I know, but why are you going?'

'It's raining.'

'I'm sorry, I don't understand, my Spanish isn't too good.'

'It's OK. I prefer my women not to speak.'

They left.

Then the rain really started to practise for England. It poured down. There was a hole in the dining room that you could drive a car through, and to add to the work for my mop and bucket, nobody had bothered to mention toilet training for dogs. Using the mobile with the dodgy connection—we didn't have a land line at the time—I called Stephen.

'The builders have gone.'

'They'll be back tomorrow.'

'There is a huge hole in the wall.'

'Not for long.'

'It's raining.'

'It'll stop.'

'Charly keeps peeing inside.'

'Take him outside.'

'But it's raining.'

'Sorry can't hear you, you're breaking up, call later, love you, bye.'

Bastard.

We had given no thought to food for our newly acquired pet. I was twenty minutes drive from town, but without a car. For three days Charly ate cornflakes for breakfast soaked overnight in milk, tuna for lunch and a jar of hot dog sausages, only a month past their sell-by date, for supper. Hot dogs are still his favourite food.

During those first six months, every other Thursday, late in the afternoon I would get a phone call.

'A story of civil war; of a quixotic battle against nature and loss;'

'No, I don't think so.'

'Harry Silver has it all: a beautiful wife, a wonderful son, a great job in the media—but one night he throws it all away.'

'Perfect. Yes please.'

'… the spare narrative hides a commitment to his subject which pulls you in and leaves you gasping.'

'Sounds a bit heavy.'

This was Stephen standing in the W H Smith's at Heathrow's Terminal Two and trying to keep me supplied with books. With no television, car or computer, a dodgy phone line seriously impeding my habitual two-hour phone calls to friends, and eight days a month on my own, I was reading more than ever.

WE LIVE HERE

For the first couple of months, life was just an extended holiday. There was no real plan for each day. Bumping into friends in town could often lead to a lunch on the beach, which would finish at about four or five, an invitation to come back for a sundowner and the day was all but gone. Fine for holidays, but we soon realised that to live here permanently and ideally to share this new life with our livers, something would have to change.

Of course, it is perfectly possible to live on the Costa del Sol without letting the fact that it happens to be in Spain intrude at all. We have met many people who do just that.

Twelve years ago, the English newspapers didn't arrive until late the following day, now most are printed in Madrid and hit the news stands along with Sur, El Diario and El Pais. There were very few supermarkets—you had to play charades in the shops to get served; very few Spanish spoke any English. There were, and still are, the delights of the brand names. The fact that the best selling brand of coffee is called Bonka, the brandy to drink with it Soberano and sliced bread is Bimbo, is only surpassed by the perfect product with which to wash one's dirty knickers - the washing powder—Colon. Now, of course, Hypermarkets abound, and you can pick up your English pension at the local post office, not, I hasten to add, that I am anywhere near to doing that. There are also probably more courses teaching the Spanish to speak English than the other way round.

I recently phoned an English friend who was full of cold, to ask if she needed anything in town. Later:

'Hi, how are you feeling? Here's the butter you wanted.'

'Oh, SPANISH butter.'

'Yes. Is that a problem?'

'No. What's it like?'

'Butter.'

'Oh.'

She has lived in Spain for eighteen years.

Like most places in the world, where there are Brits, there is snobbery too. If your car has English number plates it usually means that you are here for more than the packaged two weeks (we may talk to you). If your licence plate is actually registered here and your car has hub caps, then you probably at least own a property and come out regularly (we may invite you for drinks). Hire cars don't seem to have hub caps for some reason that I have never discovered. If you have a dog in the car, then the odds are that you live here, either that or are besotted with your pet and and have gone through all the complications necessary to bring the mutt on holiday. However, we will risk it and probably, within a week, will become life-long friends, seeing each other almost every day for at least six months until we fall out about something very important which we can't quite remember. God help you if the vehicle has Easy Car written down the side, and these days, even worse; 'Easy Car—please bring me back clean'.

In the first couple of months, with Charly installed in the car, we received more invitations from ex-pats than we could believe. Drinks, dinner, supper, lunch, pool parties, bridge evenings, golf—I will return to that one. We had thought that London had given us a good social life, but this was Hollywood comes to Spain. To be fair, we met some very charming and interesting people but decided early on that for us to get the most out of living in Spain meant living with the Spanish people and working hard to learn and embrace their culture and their language.

We were never couch potatoes in the UK, but we were office potatoes. We lived in Islington and worked in Smithfield, a stone's throw from the meat market and only a mile from home. I walked to the office once, on a Monday morning full of good intentions. It was the same morning that I had half a grapefruit and a decaffineted black coffee for breakfast, and only one cigarette before I left the house. I think it may have been early in 1995. Normally, we drove to and from the office and caught taxis to and from meetings.

But now we lived in Spain and had a dog. From Casa Rosa it is an easy but very steep walk down to the normally dry river bed. A left turn, and we walked 'upstream'on a route that many hours later would have found us in Granada.

When we started this regime, Charly was about four months old and we would walk for an hour at a gentle pace, then turn for home. Within three months we were covering the hour's walk in twenty minutes. Younger and, we had always thought, fitter friends visiting from England were left panting at the way-side. I had paid a fortune to join London gyms and hated them, but walking amongst the pink and white oleander, crushing thyme, lavender and rosemary underfoot, didn't seem like exercise. Between us we lost four stone in six months without consious effort.

LEARNING THE LANGUAGE

In 1994 we had started taking Spanish lessons after work in the office. Julia, our teacher, is actually German. She grew up in Argentina - don't ask, I never have - and was funding her way through university by teaching languages. She was a good teacher. We were bad pupils. The theory was six until seven-thirty, twice a week and then she set homework, it was like being back at school.

It felt strange that I could leave a meeting where I had just been confidently discussing a client's budget in the hundreds of thousands of pounds and within minutes, I would revert to being a twelve-year old, dredging up all the long forgotten excuses for why, yet again, I hadn't done my homework.

Lessons took place in the glass-fronted conference room, which meant that anyone passing could, and would, just pop in. Meetings ran late and often we were just too tired to concentrate. She usually took all of this with good humour and did manage to instil the basic disciplines of Spanish grammar whilst we polished off a bottle of Pata Negra, a full-bodied, red Valdepenas. Fuelled by the wine, we would have halting conversations on every subject: philosophy, the economy of Chile, women's rights. One evening, following the latest interruption, Julia banged the table in frustration.

'You two destroy all the order and discipline of my lessons. In Spain, you wouldn't even be able to buy a pair of shoes.'

A few weeks later we returned from a trip to Salamanca, as always with a present for Julia. This time it was a pair of soft suede shoes. Though she was partly right, we had certainly struggled to buy them.

Three years ago she and her delightful Chilean husband Moyses came to stay with us for a week. On their second night we invited four friends from the village to join us for supper. It was one of those occasions when everyone and everything gelled. We sat under the velvet sky with good simple food, great company, lots of wine and laughter. Then I spotted Julia at the other end of the table giggling at overhearing my conversation with Javier.

'Julia, stop it, please don't laugh at my Spanish.'

'I'm not.'

'Yes you were, I'm doing my best.'

'Your Spanish is brilliant, honestly it is, I'm really impressed, but your accent is appalling, you sound like a peasant.'

She went on to explain that we sounded like the

equivalent of very fluent English-speaking Spaniards who had learnt the language in Glasgow, for Glasgow read Frigiliana, and that she wouldn't be seen dead with us in Madrid. Whilst Julia, to her credit, had hung in there and taught us the basics years before, most of our Spanish has been picked up here in Andalucia and is therefore of the dialect known as 'Andaluz'.

Unless you are one of those irritatingly fortunate people for whom foreign languages come almost naturally, which to me they certainly do not, then you will probably have your own horror stories. My simple early mistakes, such as 'goodnight I'll have a chicken exit' to a smiling waiter, pale into insignificance beside one of my attempts at a conversation with Antonio— he of the bar—within a month or so of moving here.

He and Rosario live across the road and below the bar, at the end of a rough track. Their little house has an outside toilet and kitchen. They have a mule, an old bow-backed horse, a pig, numerous cats with their kittens, dogs with their puppies, rabbits, birds and several dozen chickens, all living so close to them that we call it Animal Farm.

It was raining on the morning that he brought the eggs. The builders had just left. Again it was only a drizzle but enough to scare off the builders and bring the men out of the fields and into the bar. The top half of our stable door was open and he leaned in with the carton of eggs.

'Hello Antonio come in out of the rain.'

'Where is your husband?'

'In England.'

'Then I will not enter, thank you. Take these. They are this morning's lay, still warm.'

'Thank you.'

He hurriedly pushed the carton into my hands and almost ran down the steps, calling out behind him that he would like the egg box back when I had the time.

Later it was explained to me that a man seen calling on a women with a gift when her husband was away was a cause for scandal.

I transferred the three eggs into a bowl they were still warm and stuck with little downy feathers. An hour or so later, having perfected my thank yous with the help of the well-worn dictionary and 501 Spanish Verbs, I returned the egg carton to the crowded, noisy bar. Any twelve people would make a bar of that size heave, and twelve Spaniards made it sound like a riot. Silence fell. Not just a woman entering the bar alone, but a foreign woman. I summoned up my perfectly rehearsed sentence as I put the carton on the bar.

'Antonio, thank you very much for giving me your beautiful big brown eggs. They look delicious, I am sure I will enjoy them.'

There was silence. At least a minute of it as I walked away. Antonio had smiled, his eyes had twinkled, but he had not said a word, then from behind me the bar shook. The laughter startled the mules tethered to the railings and made the matted mule-dogs bark with excitement. Walking back up the steps to our house I met Mayte, our good neighbour, who during her time in Paris had somehow learned a lot of English, which she liked to practise with me.

'It's raining a little. The men, they need little excuse to stop working and have fun in the bar.'

'Yes. Antonio brought me some eggs earlier. I have just returned the box. They seem to think it's funny.'

'Why? What did you say?'

'I thanked Antonio for giving me his beautiful big brown eggs, and said they looked delicious.'

'Ahh.'

'Muchas gracias para dar me tus huevos grandes y marrones, paracen deliciosos.'

'Ahh.'

'That's right, isn't it? I looked it all up.'

She smiled. 'Yes, that is right enough, but tell me, in England is there a slang or rude word for testicles?'

'Balls.'

'In Spain, it is eggs.'

WE ARE DYING TO SEE YOU

M y definition of a true friend is someone you could call at four in the morning, say 'HELP' and they would be there as soon as humanly possible, no questions asked. Someone whom you may not even see for a year or two and yet within minutes of meeting up again, it is as if you were never apart. I consider us lucky in that we have five friends of that calibre in the UK and have made four more since moving to Spain. Outside of that we knew lots and lots of people; people we liked very much, people we would see pretty regularly in London. Naturally enough, in the growing euphoria of our imminent departure we both threw out casual invitations to come and visit at every opportunity. And they came. Some even made it here before our furniture.

When the phone rang two days before the Easter holidays, Stephen was yet again at the airport picking up our latest visitors. In fact, he spent so much time there in the first two years that the airport police pulled him over to inquire about his running of an illegal taxi service.

'Hello, thought we'd let you know we are just approaching Fungi Rola.'

'Umm who IS this?.'

'Oh sorry it's Easy Move here, like, Dennis, with your furniture, like.'

'Great, so you will be here within a couple of hours.'

'A couple of minutes more like."

"We are in Frigiliana.'

'Yeah, like I just said we're really close, so like, how do we like find you, like?'

'You are the wrong side of Malaga.'

'No, we are very close to Funga Lola.'

"We are in Frigiliana, at least an hour and a bit EAST of Malaga."

'Shit. Sorry.'

When they did arrive, the darlings took one look at the steep stairs to the house, announced them to be no problem, then looked very relieved when I said that almost everything was going straight into the basement.

The friends that Stephen had just picked up at the airport, however, were an entirely different matter. Of course, people have food they don't enjoy or even can't possibly eat. For Stephen it's liver and please don't offer me tripe or anything animaly that too closely resembles the original. Outside of that, we can manage it all with a smile.

'Hi, had a good siesta? Just doing us a bit of supper. Oh, I forgot to ask, is there anything that you two don't eat?'

'I can't stomach tomatoes, onions or garlic and Damien has recently decided to cut out all fish and dairy products.'

I don't know who was more pissed off, me, or the paella simmering on the hob.

FOUR CATS AND A FUNERAL

Stephen's darling Uncle Jack died that first June and we went back for the funeral. We were only gone for three days. Arriving back at our sleepy La Molineta in the early evening, we were surprised to see at least a dozen people wandering around in the road.

A cat with her three little kittens had been living in the hay barn very happily; we had seen them several times, her babies were about three or four weeks old. I had often taken milk to the shy young mum who seemed little more than a kitten herself. She always ignored it until she thought I had gone, then wolfed the lot. For reasons known only to her, she had decided to move them. Having crossed the road once and successfully deposited a kitten in the bushes on the other side, she had been hit by a car when trying to move kitten number two. She was dead and Antonio was dealing with that side of things. Everyone else was on a kitten hunt. The little mite she had had in her mouth at the time had shot under the bonnet of Mayte's husband's, Roger's car. His solution to this, which I thought a tad drastic, was to start the engine. It worked though, and a tiny black and white bundle was quickly stuffed into a cardboard box. It was easy to find the second baby in the bushes, and in theory the remaining kitten, still in the hay stack, would not be a problem. She had other ideas. When uncovered, she shot up the nearest drainpipe and refused to be moved. A plate of tuna, a saucer of milk, lots of puss puss puss, clever girl, pretty girl. Nothing. We were, once again, back to the Roger school of cat rescue. He turned his hose on full blast and shoved it up the pipe. The kitten, now known as Pantoja, appeared with a woosh. Tiny to begin with, the smallest of the three and soaking wet, she was a pathetic sight but, mission accomplished. A drink in Antonio's seemed essential and everyone congratulated everyone on a job well done. For a full hour, I must confess, the kittens in their cardboard box were forgotten. We were all leaving when Antonio shoved the box at me.

'For you.'

'No. Antonio. No.'

'You love animals.'

'Yes, you know I do. But we have a puppy now.'

'True. Keep for tonight. Tomorrow I will sort it.'

And that is how we came to be the proud owners of Pavarotti, Picasso and Pantoja, or rather, as is almost always the case with cats, they came to own us. To name Picasso was easy. He was the black and white one with an off-centre stripe down his nose. The other two would have fooled any breeder of Siamese seal points, even down to the knobbly lumps on the ends of their tails. One was fat and, with the previous P in mind, he became Pavarotti. His almost identical but skinny little sister sang all the time, actually more of a trill than a song. Here there is a famous lady singer, Isabelle Pantoja, whose husband was a bullfighter and died in the ring, leaving her with a baby daughter. She would appear on stage with her little girl, both dressed in matching flamenco dresses, and they would sing love songs to her dead husband. As the Spanish love a good sob story, every song she released went straight to number one. So our little singer is La Pantoja- a.k.a. Issy. Not a Mediterranean tabby in sight.

LOURDES

When we bought La Panificadora and agreed to honour the rental contract until the end of October, we inherited Adora. Adora had looked after the house for more than twenty years and fulfilled the specified 'maid service twice weekly'. She saw this change of ownership as her time to retire, but did promise to find us a new cleaner.

As promised, the following Wednesday, Adora arrived to clean the Panificadora with Lourdes, her second cousin's sister-in-law's nephew's best friend's wife or some such village connection. They did a brilliant job. Stephen maintains that Frigiliana is the world academy of cleaners. Two hours later Adora reported that Lourdes understood what was required and that she would be our cleaner from now on. Lourdes Martin Martin. The Spanish take their father and mother's surnames and keep them through life; she is Martin Martin because her mother and father are first cousins. Rather posh really; everyone is always double-barrelled. She smiled shyly and they left.

Saturday, her next working day, she was sitting at the bottom of our steps at quarter-to-ten.

'Hello, Lourdes. You're early.'

'Yes. Sorry, I thought I might not get a lift, but I was lucky. Sorry.'

'It is not a problem. You were going to walk here from the village?'

'Of course.'

'Come in, have a coffee.'

We talked for a few minutes. Looking back, it now seems hard to believe that the enormous character that is Lourdes was at the time so timid. I learnt that her husband, Julio, was the local goat man with a herd of three hundred and, at the time, though now long eaten, they also had two piglets named Serrano and Iberico in anticipation of the hams! She had left school at fourteen, normal for the time, helped her mother at home and her father in the fields, until she married at eighteen and had her son the following year. This, her first job, meant her first taste of independence, the first few peseatas she was going to earn, and more importantly, the first that she could choose how to spend.

She was a five by three-foot Lycra-clad bubbly dynamo, reverse these numbers and you got her age. Her chipped and ragged fingernails were always painted a bright pink, purple or, occasionally, blue. Pale skinned for an Andalucian campo wife, she turns crimson for a week in early spring and is mahogany by mid June, although this tan, so coveted by holiday makers, never quite disguises the bites and scratches on her arms and legs that come from working with three hundred goats. She has cheap gold rings on every finger, some of which have been there for so long that, like bindings on young trees, the skin has begun to grow around them.

Five thin gold chains adorn her neck. The oldest of these bears the inscription 'Lrods ', a present from her aunt and uncle at her baptism before they had learnt to read or write. She has a passion for high heels, handbags and hair colours, too; since earning spending money she has been every shade from peroxide blonde to almost black. After a recent disastrous trip to the village hairdresser—a cousin, naturally—she arrived home bright orange, causing Julio to rave at her for spending good money to look like a gas bottle. Her stamina is as spectacular as her voice, she works like a demon, and sings like an angel.

When David, my son, was first here, he was just beginning to enjoy Spanish music.

'I wouldn't mind a copy of this one.'

'Copy of what?'

'I don't know who she is, but she's got a great voice.'

'You can't copy that, it's Lourdes, she's upstairs singing along to the radio.'

Years later she would explain how excited, delighted and terrified she was during those first few weeks.

Lourdes is the middle one of three sisters and the mother of one boy, also a Julio. It is traditional here that the first-born son is named after the father and the same applies to mothers and daughters, although all that is changing rapidly. I predict a time not so far in the future when there will probably be more native Brooklyns and Kylies in the village than Placidos or Inmaculadas.

Lourdes may never have worked before, but she certainly knew how to clean. Of course the climate helps. It is possible to douse almost everything in copious amounts of water, pop it outside for ten minutes and it is dry. This approach she applied to everything: mattresses, sofa cushions and rugs. Charly learnt very early in life that, when Lourdes was around, to stand still was to be in imminent danger of being washed.

In these early days, with only one young dog and three small kittens in the house, Lourdes would clean for us for four hours a week and then go next door to the Panificadora mid-week and on Saturdays when people were arriving and leaving to do a thorough blitz. To begin with she was very nervous about entering the Pan, especially if there were clients lying by the pool, but she quickly picked up 'Good Moaning, I am your cleaner,' and felt much more comfortable once she was able to introduce herself. We all settled into this routine.

One Saturday morning a couple of months or so later, soon after the latest clients had left, Lourdes, as usual, had gone next door to start work. Within seconds she was back.

'Jackie, there is a letter here with my name, then some English writing and some money.'

'Lourdes it is for you, it says thank you for looking after them. 'Es un consejo.' I had got it wrong again. The only word I could think of for a tip was consejo, which actually means advice, as in how to do something—I'll give you a tip. I should have used propina—a gratuitity.

She started crying.

'Why are you crying, Lourdes?'

'Before this the people did not leave money. Do all the people who were here before think that I did NOT look after them, and do they think I need money for lessons in how to clean?' Some tip, some don't,and yet again I got the words wrong.

LA PANIFICADORA

At the end of October the rental contract expired and with it my frustrations of that summer. Casa Rosa didn't have a pool, and a summer spent listening to the delighted squeals and splashings of people next door in MY pool as the temperature hit the high thirties was, shall we say, not easy.

Only having access to the house every other Saturday for four hours, I would rush in with my tape measure, fabric samples and paint charts as soon as the latest tenants had loaded their cars. But now it was ours, really ours.

The month that Paco promised it would take to strip and rebuild the kitchen turned out to be almost two, something that should have taught us a lesson for the future, but didn't at the time. So, on the twenty-first of December, the day before eight friends and family arrived for Christmas, Lourdes and I were busy dragging crates up from the basement and unpacking long-forgotten treasures.

Stephen turned up in the kitchen just as Lourdes was exclaiming her surprise that so many of the casserole dishes, pots, plates and jugs were exactly like the ones from around here. She had thought they would have been very different, having come from England. He rolled his eyes, grunted and left. For more than ten years we had never left Spain without armfuls of rustic pottery, sometimes paying excess baggage for the privilege. Now we had paid again to bring them all home.

Home. Home. Home. At last I was home. My father was a lifetime army man with the Royal Scots, which meant that we had moved a lot. In fact, we moved from Pennicuck to Colchester in the ten days around my birth. Ten days, the time then spent in hospital to 'dar luz' (to give light), the Spanish expression for giving birth. My mother had waddled out of one house in Southern Scotland and carried me back into another in Southern England. Six months later we were in Germany. It seemed to set a pattern that continued for many years.

Now was going to be so different, so permanent. La Panificadora, with its walled and terraced gardens, trickling water, arches and mill stones, its views of sea and mountains. Its newly designed kitchen, to me the perfect blend of modern appliances hidden behind rustic doors and with tons of space for friends to sit and chat whilst we cooked. I would never, ever, move again.

CHARLY GROWS UP

We revelled in the luxury of lie-ins and, unless we had builders arriving, nine a.m. would often find us sipping coffee, sitting on the terrace still wrapped in towelling robes and planning the day ahead. Charly was a good dog, something that we told him often and that he always seemed pleased to hear.

Stephen had searched for dog-training books on his first trip back to London and, being in a rush as usual, had gone for two extremes. One advised that man was the master and that the puppy had to learn this at an early stage. It also had lots of instructions about using rolled-up newspapers to practically beat the poor thing into submission and cages to keep it confined. The other was entitled 'Never say No' and recommended that every animal deserved to have the time and space to find and express its own personality. Saying 'No' may restrict the animal's ability to 'project itself' it claimed. Charly was my first dog, but not my first child, and in child rearing I had found that 'No' was a very useful word. On the other hand though, I had never used a rolled up newspaper or a cage—except, perhaps, a playpen. Both books went in the rubbish bin and we followed our instincts.

For months one or the other of us walked with Charly first thing every morning to the top of the track that led down to the river. He would then run off, do what he had to do, and be sitting outside our door waiting to be let in within ten or fifteen minutes. One Sunday, he didn't return. After two hours Stephen walked down to the river bed but there was no sign of him. After four hours Stephen drove around looking for him. Nothing. I walked half way back down the rough track to the river and stopped at Jose and Adela's house to ask if they had seen him. Not only had Adela not seen Charly but her little dog, Bobby, a pal of Charly's, had also gone out that morning and not returned. We went to bed very late that night reassuring each other that he was bound to be fine, that he had probably just got distracted by an interesting smell. We both got up several times when we thought the other was asleep, to see whether he was sitting on our steps. He wasn't.

Late the next morning Adela knocked on our door in floods of tears and with an incredible story. In town that morning she had been stopped in the street by a woman she didn't know who told her that both Charly and her little Bobby had been stolen. They were being kept in a basement in Calle Granada, one of the smartest residential streets in Nerja, by foreigners who were going to take Bobby back to France for medical experiments. But they had decided that they didn't want Charly, they were only keeping him to keep Bobby quiet and were going to kill him before they left. She said the woman then ran off before she could stop her.

We couldn't make sense of what we were hearing. It just seemed so far fetched, but by the time she had finished, I too, was crying. That evening Stephen went to see Adela's husband Jose to suggest that they both go and knock on every door in Calle Granada to try to find foreigners that might be living there and that might have a basement. Jose, looking very embarrassed, told Stephen that he was sure they would be wasting their time, just as Adela had already wasted their money. The truth was that she had not been stopped in the street as she said, but she had been too embarrased to admit that she had gone to the local adivina (white witch) and paid her to tell what had happened to the dogs by reading the cards. We were both astounded and relieved. But Charly was still missing.

For the following five days our lives were ruled by Charly's absence. Armed with a photo, Stephen toured the myriad tracks around here for hours at a time stopping to ask anyone and everyone if they had seen him. I wouldn't leave the house in case there was any news. By the following Friday, with little hope, I joined him as he set off yet again. After four hours and at least five miles from home, we turned back and began to face the fact that our search was becoming increasingly futile. Minutes later, Stephen was driving and I was still hanging out of the side window calling Charly's name in a voice that by this time was almost hoarse.

'Charly, there you are.'

'Stephen, don't joke. This is not bloody funny.'

Then I looked ahead. Lying by the side of the road a few yards in front of us were two exhausted dogs, both filthy. It took me a few seconds to realise that one of them was ours, then I was out of the car before it had stopped.

The ugly bitch that had tempted him away (of course I am only using the correct term for a female dog here) was, in truth, one of the ugliest bitches I had ever seen. As instructed, Charly got into the car, although he looked less than delighted to see us. In a moment of madness Stephen suggested that we take the girlfriend too.

'Are you insane?'

'Well, she's probably going to have Charly's puppies.'

'Exactly. In fact, she's almost definitely going to have Charly's puppies. Just drive, please, just drive.'

We took him home and he walked up the steps like John Wayne. We hosed him down, removed at least a dozen ticks, covered him in flea powder and gave him a lecture about safe sex and his poor taste in women. He ate, went to his basket and slept for forty-eight hours with a big smile on his face. Luckily the canine version of the Child Support Agency has never caught up with us. Bobby found his own way home safely later that same day.

SYBIL

Sybil lived above us in a charming little cottage, El Huerto (The Orchard) with a beautiful garden reached by about fifty yards of steep dirt track. She was in her late eighties when we first met. One of the first women to go to Cambridge, she then went into the diplomatic service, had travelled the world and was still prone to wonderful one-liners such as; 'Darling, Moscow in the thirties was a hoot. We were starving, of course, but vodka cost peanuts.'

She was apparently married for a short time in her late twenties, but dismissed it as 'a state that didn't agree with her'. Two black and white photographs and an oil painting in her living room gave proof to the fact that she was a stunner in her day. She was 'at home' between four and five-thirty every weekday and always dressed for the occasion, in slightly faded, care- fully darned cashmere twin sets, pearls, a smudge of pale pink lipstick, baby blue eyeshadow and a splash of Chanel No 5. She would then sit on her terrace and watch for anyone coming up the track, although we never saw anyone else visit.

She died before we moved here permanently, but whilst on holiday I would visit her almost every day and often do her shopping. Once, she had batteries on her shopping list, batteries for the little radio that she kept beside her bed, though when I replaced the old with the new I could not tune it. Most efficiently, she found the dog-eared instruction manual and, deciding that it was definitely a 'boy thing' I went to find Stephen.

'Sybil says that she only needs three channels, the local radio, Madrid Classical and the BBC World Service.'

'OK. Won't take a minute.'

For almost two hours Stephen muttered and swore. The radio was finally programmed. It was, of course, the fault of the badly translated Japanese manual that it had taken so long!

'Right, here we go, I've written it down for Sybil. Button One; Local Radio, Button Two; Madrid Classical and the BBC World Service is on Three.'

'Sybil, sorry it took so long, but here we are, Stephen has written it all down for you, look.'

She looked at the piece of paper and then,

'Well, thank you, my dear girl, but it's not possible that the BBC is on Three, it has always always been on One.'

'Well, it's on button Three now, Sybil, working perfectly, and your other two stations are on One and Two.'

'Bloody BBC! They must have changed their wavelength without telling anyone, it's appalling, in fact, it's a scandal. I know the Director General, had cocktails with him on many occasions, I shall write immediately. I probably didn't even need new batteries.'

No amount of persuasion would convince her that this was not the case. In the end I gave up and left her rummaging through drawers to find the address she was looking for.

DOMINGO

———

I still don't know where time goes here, now almost eight years have skipped by. That first March till Christmas just disappeared. Charly grew in many ways apart, that is, from his ears which have never changed from the day we got him. To begin with they hung to his chin, looking promisingly like those of a Spanish Pointer, but over the months as his head got bigger they didn't and instead they became small fly-away afterthoughts on the side. He dug a hole in the garden, a hole at least a foot deep between the roots of the jacaranda tree, and on the rare occasions that he was in trouble he would go and sit in it, hiding his head between his paws. We called this hole his Trophy Cupboard. We always knew where to find anything that went missing: shoes, books, pens, tea towels and he was particularly fond of my bras. Never chewed, just saved in Charly's Trophy Cupboard.

We were beginning to take for granted the fact that

we woke to sunshine every morning. Unless we were going out, shorts, shirts and flip-flops were all that were necessary. One morning in the second week of November—I remember the date well, the eleventh, Stephen's birthday, Charly started barking loudly. This was unusual. He never was and indeed still isn't a very vocal dog. His preferred style of communication is usually a sort of short chuff that makes the wobbly bits at the side of his mouth, well, wobble.

The barking continued and we went to investigate. He was standing in the middle of the terrace and it had started to rain, big slow fat plops that splashed on to the thirsty sun baked terracotta tiles and spread mysteriously. He pawed at the tiles as he would an insect, but was driven indoors when a drop landed on his nose. It took us a moment to realise that, like us, he had taken the sunshine for granted, though, unlike us, he was too young to remember the last time it had rained.

Of course had the opportunity to acquire a Spanish pointer arisen we would certainly have been very tempted, but with three cats the idea of Mediterranean tabbies was definitely on a very back burner. In fact, we had decided that one dog was enough. Charly came everywhere with us, he was trained to sit, stay, walk to heel without a lead and not to touch food without our permission.

On the fourth of January, with Charly at our side, we went to Antonio's for a drink. In Spain, the early days of January are a bit of time in limbo. Christmas officially starts on the eighth of December with the feast of the Immaculate Conception. I was brought up in a typical Catholic family and, when old enough to notice such things, I was very impressed that Mary was only pregnant for seventeen days. There must be a God. It seemed to take normal women and even my rabbit much longer than that.

Christmas Eve, Noche Buena, is celebrated with a big family meal and then after the midnight mass the party continues until dawn. There is an old Spanish saying : Esta Noche es Noche Buena, y no es noche de dormir. (This is the good night and not the night for sleep.) Christmas Day is relatively quiet, a time for church services, religious reflections and the nursing of hangovers.

There are big parties in the Plaza de La Iglesia on New Year's Eve when, according to village tradition, it is very important that the women wear red knickers to ensure luck in the coming year. Nobody has been able to even begin to explain why, although I suspect it is a tradition that was linked to fertility. Then as the church tower rings out the first bell of midnight every-one tries to eat twelve grapes before the last chime, which is a lot more difficult than it sounds.

The New Year's Eve that moved 1998 into 1999 cer-tainly had links to fertility in Frigiliana. The electricity had been going on and off all evening, but just after eleven it packed up for the night. The celebrations in the Plaza were cancelled, the bars and restaurants closed and, although dressed in their best and ready for a long party, everyone went home. For weeks people bemoaned the fact that it had been one of the least celebrated new years that they could remember. Five or six months later however, it became very apparent that private celebrations had continued, and the following late September early October, twenty-two babies were born. When they started school, three years later, it was the first time in the history of the village that they had two entry-year classes.

The present-giving that we associate with Christmas Day is not until the sixth of January, Dia De Los Reyes, The Day of the Kings. It is only the eager greed of our modern society that celebrates the birth of Christ with presents on the 25th. On the night of the fifth of January all the children in the village put their shoes on their doorsteps filled with carrots and straw for the three king's horses, and are rewarded with presents the following day. Consequently, although there are probably ten Spanish working days from early December till mid January, none of them are really taken very seriously. It is one very long holiday.

So, once again we took the sixty second walk to Antonio's and the bar was full of 'workers' on their way home. Rosario, still firmly ensconced in our basement every night, was of course accepted in the bar as the wife of Antonio. Female foreigners, after walking in the mountains, occasionally stopped for drinks; that has now become the norm. But for a local woman even if she is not Spanish and is also accompanied by her husband the etiquette is to sit with Rosario quietly in a corner. Sitting quietly in the corner talking to Rosario, I watched as Placido arrived on his battered old scooter and ordered his usual vino de terreno, the local sweet Malaga wine that had caused me so much damage on the night that I had offered to sort out the puppy problem some nine months before. I have not touched it since. I listened with half an ear to the background conversation, whilst enjoying Rosario's many stories of her recent bi-annual trip to Malaga.

'I'll be back, I just need to get rid of this... I don't suppose you need a new dog, do you, Antonio?'

'What do you think.'

'No. OK. I'll be back in a minute.'

Stephen stopped Placido on his way out of the bar and asked to look at the dog.

From his inside jacket pocket Placido lifted a tiny puppy and passed it over to Stephen. It sat, blinking and terrified, in the palm of his hand.

'He would have been a good dog, from this mother they always have been, she always has good dogs. But he is the smallest of the three, and she is old and tired now; this is her seventh litter. She has little milk these days and can only just manage to feed two.'

'So what are you going to do with him?'

'Put him down the acequia.'

'Drown him?'

'What else. No one will take him. What else can I do? It will be a quicker death than starving.'

I could hear it coming.

'JACKIE.'

It was a Sunday. We took him from a gentle kind man who deserved his name, Placido, and by then we already had a cat called Pavarotti. This dog had to be a Domingo. We assured each other that one more very small dog wouldn't make any difference. Like children, two can be less trouble than one, and such good company for one another. I tucked him inside my jacket. He grunted softly and fell asleep.

Domingo, our second dog to be introduced to the vet. Again it was Rafael, professional, polite, yet, when working, short on charm to humans, but full of love for animals.

He went through the usual checks. Then.

'You have children?'

'I have a son, yes, but he is grown up now.'

'Good. You still remember four-hourly feeds?'

'God, yes.'

'Good. You feed this every four hours for the next two weeks or he will most certainly die. He is probably not yet three weeks old, a little undernourished perhaps, but he is, in general, I think, quite healthy.'

I stifled the temptation to rush out and buy blue babygrows and a wicker crib and instead set about the less romantic and more practical task of bottle feeding a very tiny puppy. He would not eat. He gagged on the teat. Every time I got it near his mouth he threw his head from side to side with impressive force, but he grew weaker by the hour. In desperation, just before midnight, I called and woke my mum in England.

She was born and raised on a farm and was of the 'no nonsense' school.

'Cut your little finger nail as short as you possibly can. I am presuming here that your nails are still as ridiculous as ever?'

'They are sort of longish.'

'Exactly. Cut it off, file it smooth, then try and put your finger as flat as possible into some warm milk with just the tip above the milk and encourage him to suck it. Wring out a warm wet flannel and stroke the back of his head with this at the same time. It replicates the mother's tongue. Oh, and wrap a small clock in a towel and put it beside him when you put him down to sleep; he will think it is his mother's heartbeat. Call back tonight if you have a problem. I'll sleep on the settee in case you do. Good Luck darling.'

It worked. Within a minute or two he didn't even need my little finger. He had learned to lap and wanted more and more warm milk, so much so that as it was going in at one end it began to come out at the other. It was a huge relief, but not the end of the road. It was still party season and Spanish parties never last for less than four hours. He had to come with us. I dug out an old esparto grass bag with long leather handles, the type the local women use for carrying vegetables back from the market, and in my party finery slung this over my shoulder wherever we went. Inside, swaddled in a towel, lying on a hot water bottle was little Domingo. The bars of the village, always very accommodating to people with young children, were surprised, amused and helpful. He thrived and soon grew into one of those dogs we swore we would never have, the typical short stocky Andalucian village dog whose tail curls over his back. He was good with the cats. It helped that they were much bigger than him for the first few months, in fact Pavarotti still is. At times he could be a little over enthusiastic. I have often wondered what the people holidaying next door in Casa Rosa thought when overhearing my plea, 'Domingo, how many times have I told you - don't do that to Pavarotti.'

It was not long until we could take away the bricks we had put on the garden steps to help him to follow Charly everywhere. They were and they still are inseparable.

THE HONOURABLE PIG

The following Sunday we were invited to Antonio's house for lunch. His sons, Antonio and Paco, and their sister Maria, were all going to be there with their families; it was to be a big event. We accepted with pleasure until...

'Jackie, I am killing the pig in your honour.'

'The pig? You're killing it?'

'Yes. In your honour.'

'Antonio, no. No, it's a lovely pink pig, thank you very much, but I would be much more honoured if it lived.'

He thought this a good joke.

At nine on Sunday morning he banged on the door. There is no mistaking Antonio's knock. He ignores the beautiful hand of Fatima and instead uses his own gnarled fist of Antonio. Stephen answered in his dressing-gown.

'That was Antonio. The butcher has arrived and is ready to kill the pig.'

'Oh, how sad.'

'They are waiting for you.'

'Me? Why?'

'Because it is being killed in your honour. You have to be there.'

'No way. We have been through all this. You know how I hate it.'

'Tough, they are waiting for you.'

'Make an excuse. I'm ill or something.'

'No.'

I summoned up my best look. Thank God it worked and Stephen padded off to make my excuses, assuring Antonio that I would be fine very soon and we would be there by two at the latest.

Rosario's house, for the bar is Antonio's and the house Rosario's, is always a delight. She begs, borrows and, yes, probably acquires plant cuttings from everyone around here. She uses old olive oil cans and paint drums as flower pots. The result is a picturesque Spanish version of Steptoe's yard. Built on the steep hillside, the only token gestures to safety are the many old doors and rusted bed bases stacked up at the edge of the kitchen that stop you falling a good fifty feet into the avocado trees below.

Inside the tiny house there are numerous statues of Jesus and the Virgin Mary. Vases are laden with pink plastic roses with plastic water drops on their petals, hand-crocheted antimacassars adorn every chair and the similar mats on every surface are topped by much prized official photos of christenings, first communions and weddings. It is only possible to navigate that living room with a sideways step.

We arrived just before two at a scene from the Texas Chainsaw Massacre. There were bits of pig everywhere. The women, Rosario, her daughter Maria and the two daughters-in laws were scraping bits of meat from skin and bone, then mixing the result with lots of paprika, chopped garlic, handfuls of stale breadcrumbs and stuffing it into the intestines, which had been soaked for an hour or two in milk, to make Chorizo sausage. I now understand the origin of the expression 'Up to your arms in it'. My honourable pink pig was skinned and pinned to a door by its forelegs, his pose rather resembling some of Rosario's statues inside the house. Miss this next bit if, like me, you are squemish. I closed my eyes when I typed it.

The butcher was carving great slabs of meat from the haunches and passing them to Paco who was layering them in huge rubber buckets and throwing handfuls of sea salt between each layer. The old washing-up bowl underneath caught most of the blood which was saved to make morcilla, a spicy version of black pudding. But the bowl didn't catch it all and I noticed that when Rosario got up to fetch more bread, her foam slippers left squelchy bloody footprints in her wake. The older men were focusing on the eyes, ears, brain, trotters and the tongue, having a heated argument about the preferred preservation of such delicacies. When a bucket of meat was full it was topped off with olive oil and wrestled down to the cool store room under the house. This was to be the whole family's meat for the coming year.

Meanwhile the makeshift barbeque, a piece of corrugated iron propped on some broken bricks, began to glow. The griddle was brushed with dark green olive oil and sprigs of rosemary were shoved between the burning pine logs. Wafer-thin slices of pork began to sizzle and spit, fresh bread was cut, red local wine was poured, and - in my honour—I was offered the first piece of meat.

I turned my back to the family and looked frantically at Stephen.

'I can't do this.'

'Course you can.'

'Can't.'

'You have to. Turn round, face everyone, big smile, big bite, OK.'

'OK.'

Just as I turned, faced everyone, big smile about to take big bite, the butcher choose that exact moment to decapitate the pig.

Luckily, Stephen caught me.

WATER SLIDES

Unlike Charly, it was probably a good six weeks before Domingo had his first proper car journey, other than that first trip to the vet. They were both in the back of the car on the way to their walk on the beach. Quite understandably most of the beaches have now banned dogs, but there are still a few, off the beaten track, where it is possible to let them run, and they love it. Stephen was driving and I was looking over my shoulder and laughing at the way that the little one was trying to copy Charly. With his back legs on the arm rest, he was at full stretch to get his nose out of the back window, which was about a third open.

'He's safe, isn't he? I mean, he couldn't fall out.'

'Of course not, don't worry, he's fine.'

'STOP THE CAR!'

'What?'

'Domingo's gone! He's not there!'

'Don't be stupid.'

Stephen pulled over and we searched the Land Rover in vain. He was not there. With impressive speed I was hysterical. With impressive calm Stephen took charge. I was to walk back to where we had last seen him in the car two, certainly no more than three minutes before. He would drive. And so it was that I came to be running up and down the Spanish version of a country lane on a Saturday evening in early spring shouting 'Domingo, Domingo'. 'Sunday, Sunday.' Is it surprising the locals think we are mad? I did two laps on foot calling out to the men working in the fields asking if they had found a puppy with a red collar and expecting at any minute to find a little beige splat of a pancake on the road.

We swopped. I drove and Stephen took Charly on his lead and walked the same route. The theory was that Charly would be keen and useful in trying to find his little brother. The reality was that Charly enjoyed the walk and showed no interest or concern for Domingo. On lap three an old man waved me down.

'I've got your puppy, he's in the back of my van.'

'Thank you. Is he all right?'

'Yes, he's fine. He was in the acequia, but if it wasn't for the sluice gate he would be in the Mediterranean by now and on his way to Africa.'

Domingo was fine. Soggy, but fine. With odds of millions to one, he must have fallen from the car window straight into the water channel. The water is quite shallow, but fast running and the sides of the acequia are steep. He had travelled for at least a mile. Thoughts of a walk on the beach were long gone; we went home, dried him off, and had a therapeutic brandy.

SAN SEBASTIAN
AND SAN ANTONIO

Contrary to popular belief, most Spaniards do work as hard as they play, although there does always seems to be the time and reason or excuse for a party. As I have said, Christmas isn't over until the 6th of January, then on the 20th comes the fiesta of San Sebastian, the patron saint of Frigiliana. Actually, one of their two, but he is the original. January weather cannot be guaranteed, not good news for the parades and picnics that accompany a Saint's day. So early last century the village simply adopted San Antonio whose day is the 13th of June and much more likely to promise, in fact almost guarantee, good weather. Thus probably two-thirds of the village men are called Antonio and many of the rest are Sebastian.

On the 20th San Sebastian is decked with flowers, taken out of the church and, following Mass, is carried round the village on the men's shoulders as the sun sets. To carry the saint is an honour and a right passed from father to son, or if necessary from uncle to nephew. The fiesta is a relatively subdued affair, people are still recovering from the excesses of Christmas and I always think of Sebastian as our second class saint.

The fiesta of San Antonio, on the other hand, is the village's biggest annual event. Our house is beside the road that leads up to the village from the coast, the only road, so everything on its way to Frigiliana passes our kitchen window. The first attraction arrives about a week before the 13th: The funfair, a charmingly old fashioned collection of dodgems, coconut shies, bouncy castles and trampolines. There are shooting galleries, house of horror rides and the test-your-strength machines so very popular with spotty teenage boys trying to show off to the gaggles of giggling young girls. Food stalls offer the usual hot dogs and hamburgers along with the more traditional fiesta food of spit-roast chicken. At the end of the night, at four or five in the morning, many revellers need a sugar fix and it is time for churros and hot chocolate. Churros are squiggles of a doughnut-like batter squeezed from a fat nozzled icing tube directly into a bubbling cauldron of spitting oil. Served in a poke, like chips, they are sprinkled with sugar and washed down with thick strong dark hot chocolate. If you find it a bit rich, you can slap it directly onto your hips and thighs, achieving the same end result, but without the enjoyment. By mid-June the night-time temperature is often in the high twenties, so nothing gets going until well after ten. Then the whole village, dressed in their Sunday best, start to arrive, three sometimes four generations of one family promenading through the streets, stopping to chat with friends and watch the fun.

On the first night there is the annual Miss Frigiliana competition open to all the village girls who have their sixteenth birthday that year, and which attracts an average of ten to twelve entrants. Billed to start at ten, it sometimes manages to get going before midnight. The girls first appear in Day Wear, always jeans, white T shirts emblazoned with the name of their sponsor, Bar Al Andaluz, Fruteria Jimenez, and the obligitory platform-soled trainers. This is followed by my favourite, 'Traditional Dress' the beautiful, vibrantly coloured frilly flamenco dresses; they wear roses in the hair and have shawls casually draped around bronzed shoulders. Then, finally, 'Evening Wear' turning it into the Miss Jailbait competition. A huge team of local experts are invited to judge this prestigious event. The village hairdresser, the garage owner, last year's winner and serveral councillors from the town hall.

'Who do you think will win, Lourdes?'

'Well, number seven is really beautiful, is she not? Number three is my neighbour's daughter, Miriam, and I know that they spent a fortune on her dress; that would be nice, but I think it will be number eleven.'

'Eleven! No chance.'

'We will see.'

And the winner is... Number eleven.

'I don't believe it. Who is she, the mayor's daughter?'

'No, no, said Lourdes,' far too quickly, 'the mayor only has sons. Number eleven is his niece.'

On the thirteenth of June we all follow San Antonio down to the river. From nine in the morning, the horses brought from the campo begin to trot past our windows on their way up to the village. The men wear black and grey striped trousers, startched white shirts, red cumberbunds and black Cordoban hats. Their horses gleam, their manes and tails plaited with green and white ribbons, the colours of Andalucia. In the village, the women, also dressed in the traditional way, join them, seated sidesaddle behind the riders with the frills of their dresses spread out over the horses' rumps. The flowers in their hair are more than just decoration. They are worn behind your left ear if you are 'available', the right, if you are 'spoken for' and on top of your head if you are considered too young for such things. One year I watched with amusement as three girls of about fourteen left their house with their flowers firmly pinned on the tops of their heads. As they disappeared around the corner their flowers were swiftly being moved to behind left ears.

After a midday mass, San Antonio leaves the church. Again he is carried on the shoulders of the men in the village who are honoured to be chosen for the task. He tours the village before being transferred to an ox cart, preceded by the local municipal band, mainly teenagers. They break rank at every opportunity and rush into the crowd to greet their friends, destroying any semblance of solemnity.

Then come the riders and the floats. Every conceivable vehicle is decorated with paper chains and palm leaves and has music playing as loudly as possible. Scooters, cars, tractors and, more recently, fork-lifts and dumper trucks, a sign of the times, they all join the procession. In front of everything walks a man with a quiver of rockets slung over one shoulder. Every few minutes he sets one off, startling the horses, making tourists jump, and small children and babies cry. The noise is incredible.

From the village, this motley procession takes the twisting, almost vertical track that runs from behind the Guardia Police Station down to the river. The picnic site, in a pine wood, is about a two-mile rough trek upstream. The pink and white oleander are in full bloom and the smell of pine resin and wild herbs is heady. By June there is little water in the river and many people walk alongside the procession. Cars regularly get stuck and laughing people run to put a shoulder behind them.

By about two in the afternoon most have arrived. Cool boxes are unpacked and rugs spread under the trees. The elder children are set to work damming the river to provide a paddling pool for the little ones who without ceremony are stripped to their knickers and encouraged to play in the water.

Food, as always around here, is a joy to be shared. Andalucia in the days of Franco and before tourism was perhaps the poorest region of Spain. Yet instead of fostering a spirit of 'look out for yourself', it seems that quite the reverse has happened, and never more so than on this day. Families pride themselves on their specialities: Patricia's tortilla, Rosa's ensalada de tomate y cebolla. Paco's sardines, skewered on to pine twigs bathed in sea salt and cooked on an open fire. Not ever daring or presuming to compete with local fare, my eggy mayo and cress sandwiches are now, suprisingly, one of the big hits. So everyone sets out their offerings at their base camp and the parade begins. Essential to this is the copita, a sherry-style glass strung on a leather thong worn around the neck. Volume is still on high as people call to each other to come share a glass or a bite of something. During the course of the afternoon your copita will hold local homemade wine, manzanilla (the very dry almost salty sherry from Sanlucar de Barrameda near Jerez, the traditional drink for Feria throughout Andalucia). Then towards the end of the day, brandy.

These days the music traditionally provided by guitars and castanets comes from a local band. Everyone dances. The provision of power to the picnic site, a tenuous run of cables, has also given rise to a bar set up for just that one day serving ice-cold beer. A few years ago, we even had a giant television screen. That year on the thirteenth of June, Spain were playing Nigeria in the quarter finals of the world cup, I'm talking football here, and there was not a man in the village prepared to miss the match and go down to the river. The women rebelled. The beauty of such a small community is that people's actions can and do make a difference. A petition was duly drawn up, signed, with over three hundred female signatures, and presented to the mayor. It stated that quite simply if the men did not go to the river nor would the women and children. If nobody went it would be an insult to San Antonio and a disgrace to the village and to the church for not celebrating their Saint's day. That is how we ended up with the incongruous sight of a thirty-foot television screen, installed and paid for by the town hall, amongst the pine trees. That year the women had won the day, but Spain lost the match.

NIÑA

As the nights drew in late that Autumn, we called upon yet another Antonio, Antonio de La Lena, the woodman, to bring us our winter firewood. By this time we had tried several sources but Antonio and his son, Antonio, provided the best mix. Thin slivers of silver-grey almond wood, cut and stored from the previous spring and perfect for kindling, the pine still full of resin that gives off a wonderful smoke when burnt, and olive, dark and heavy, a dampened olive log will keep the fire smouldering all night. It was to be our second winter here and our first with the woodburning stove; it took us a while to get to know it. When we began to feel the warmth of the day fading at around six, we would light the fire. Three hours later it was doing what it had promised, by which time we were sitting under copious layers of blankets and duvets. If, mid-afternoon, it crosses your mind that you may need a fire that evening—that is the time to light it.

Charly and Domingo were in heaven. Domingo seemed to take a personal interest in selecting the wood. As soon as Stephen picked up the log basket, Domingo was beside him. Whilst the basket was loaded in our basement, he looked on, full of self-importance, sniffing each piece, then watched intently as the fire was laid and lit. I swear that by now if I asked Domingo to pop out and light the fire he would—if he could. He has become known as our Fire Monitor. Meanwhile, I would lay an old blanket in front of the hearth and that would be the two of them settled for the night.

Late one early December evening, Stephen was watching football and I was sitting at the table wrapping Christmas presents and feeling rather smug at being so far ahead of the game. The local restaurant had just closed, it was pouring with rain and a strong, very cold east wind—the Levante—was doing its worst. Andalucian houses just aren't designed for cold Levantes with their peculiar way of twisting around buildings, screaming through the smallest gaps in doors and windows and rattling the shutters. Above this noise I thought I heard something else.

'Stephen, there's a funny noise outside.'

'What sort of funny?'

'Don't know. Come and listen.'

We listened. We peered out of the window but could see nothing and settled back to present-wrapping and football-watching. Ten minutes later I was still swearing that I could hear something above the wind and, knowing me of old, Stephen faced the fact that I was not going to let this drop until he had been out to have a look.

'Your were right. There's a dog out here.'

'It must be soaking.'

'Of course it is. It's shivering. I'll bring it in.'

'NO. Charly and Domingo will go crazy.'

'OK. I'll leave it.'

'NO.'

'What then?'

'I don't know.'

'We are coming in.'

Bless him. He was soaked, shivering and with his hair plastered to his head. So I gave him a towel and turned to the dog. From that first moment and until this day, she—as she turned out to be—was heartbreakingly grateful for everything we did for her. We dried her in front of the fire, gave her food and clean water and then just sat talking gently to her. Charly had checked her out the minute she had arrived and, nature being what it is, was strutting around the room trying to look like a casual Don Juan but actually managing more of a clumsy Hugh Grant. Domingo, after the first sniff, went to his basket, put his head under his paws, and stayed there till morning.

'Jackie. We don't need another dog. We have two, it's enough.'

'I know, of course it's enough. We can't possibly keep her.'

'She is probably just lost, though she doesn't have a collar.'

'Yes, I'm sure she's just lost. I'll phone Coastline Radio tomorrow, ask if they will put out a message.'

'Good idea.'

'Sweet, isn't she?'

'We can't have another dog.'

'I know. We have agreed that. Sweet, isn't she?'

I did phone the radio station and they put out an appeal. Even better than that, I told Lourdes to ask around in the village, achieving much more coverage than local radio. I asked all the neighbours. The people running the restaurant said they had been feeding her with scraps every night for more than a week. Whilst we were waiting for her owners to turn up it seemed only wise to make our next visit to Rafael. After all, I argued, we didn't want our two catching anything that she might have and whilst there, it seemed silly not to take advantage of their special Christmas offer on dog baskets. She had been sleeping on an old towel for almost three weeks.

The night that we took her in and discovered she was a she, I started to refer to her as Niña. It means little girl and was, of course, only a temporary name. Niña she is. The closest I can describe to a breed are connections to golden spaniel. She has partially webbed feet, no tail—naturally so, it hasn't been docked—and she loves water. All water. Weeks later, Stephen was again watching football and I was soaking in a very expensive bubbly bath, head back and totally relaxed when splash, Niña was in. She sat there—I swear with a smile on her face—as if she always did this on a Saturday night. At least she had the tap end. We have a huge American-style fridge with a water dispenser on the front. It is not plumbed in, rather it has a flask in the door which takes five litres of bottled water. We are both big water drinkers and it was usual for me to top up the flask every day. Suddenly we were using far more than normal. One morning I watched as Niña wandered into the kitchen, sniffed with disdain at the dog's freshly topped-up water bowl, went over to the fridge, stood up on her back legs and used a front paw to push the dispenser lever. Turning her head to one side she drank greedily the chilled, bottled mountain spring water that she had obviously acquired quite a taste for.

Nowadays, in summer she does two laps of the pool every morning before breakfast and then drinks from the hose pipe as we water the garden. Her front left paw is at right angles to its leg, so when we want to talk about her without her hearing her name we call her 'my left foot'. We never have found out where she came from.

WE NEED A PROJECT

Rodrigo, another of those large characters who seem to flourish in this tolerant land, is a Colombian Jack of all trades, someone we met soon after moving here and thereafter bumped into pretty regularly. At one point he had a restaurant, at another an antiques business and he always had a new plan. We would occasionally have a drink with him and enjoy his company. Five years ago his thing of the moment was a stall at the Sunday morning Rastro, a mixture between a car boot fair and an antiques market. It is where foreigners try to sell things I would be ashamed to put out with the rubbish, and where the locals offer anything they deem to be old-fashioned but to us are often absolute treasures and bargains.

That particular morning we had been to look at a little house for sale in the village. It was very charming but fully restored and we were looking for a project, something for us to work on. There were two reasons for buying: it seemed foolhardy to leave all our fortunes in the hands of the stockmarket, and Spanish property prices were beginning to rise rapidly. Using Stephen's skills as an archtitect to restore an old house and then put it on the holiday rental market would keep our income in pace with inflation and hopefully give us some capital growth. It made good financial sense. Second, it would give structure and purpose to our days, and, best of all, provide an excuse to visit the antique shops, junk yards and obscure little craft work shops tucked away in the tiny villages that we both enjoy so much.

When Rodrigo learnt that we may possibly be in the 'property market' as he grandly called it, he insisted that we look at the house of his friend's wife in the next village.

This was a project. The terraced house is in the middle of Calle Real, the main street of the sleepy little village of Maro, no more than two miles east of Nerja. It had belonged to Rodrigo's friend's wife's mother. She had died many years earlier and the tiny house had been closed the following day; her daughter could not bear to enter —too many memories.

It was suspended in time. In the kitchen a paper calendar, showing July 1973, was hanging by a nail from the flaking limestone wall. Even the bats that hung from the rafters didn't look that pleased with their squat. We began to climb the stairs then someone shouted that it wasn't safe. From half way up we could see the large single room ahead of us with a fireplace in the corner. The bed was still made up:

sheets, pillows and a hand-stitched quilt. A water glass
and a pair of wire-rimmed spectacles were on an old
wooden chest by the bed and a pair of ladies' slippers sat neatly placed on the floor beside it. The roof
had almost completely collapsed and much of it had
landed on the bed.

But, as usual, outside it was a beautiful day and the
sky looked azure through the gap. Beyond the back
door was a paved yard broken by jungle-sized weeds
ending in a pile of rubble that had once apparently
been home to the mule. Rodrigo pointed out the worn
path from front door to back in the terracotta tiles
which was the result of many years of walking the
mule in and out through the house every night and
every morning. There was also a lean to, a toilet facil-
ity at its most basic which I viewed from a distance. I
was wondering how Stephen was going to get us out
of this politely.

'It needs a lot of work.'

Rodrigo and his friend shrugged.

'A new roof, of course, and a lick of paint.'

'More than that, how much are you asking?'

Why even ask? I was amazed. Polite is one thing,
but PLEASE. I opened my mouth to speak. We have
learnt over time that when talking to each other with
Spanish friends around, many of whom speak at least
some English, slang can be very useful.

'Button up.'

I buttoned.

To be fair, the price they mentioned was very very

low, but by this stage I would have paid almost that just to leave. I can only button for so long and, knowing this, Stephen said he would 'think about it' and we left.

Maro has a great tapas bar and we went there for lunch. Its reputation is built on excellent seafood. We ordered mussels, just plain steamed, so fresh it would be an insult to add anything. Flash-fried fresh boquerones, which are actually anchovies, but nothing like the salty things that come with pizzas, more like baby sardines. Almejas, tiny clams cooked in a garlic sauce, and rosada, the local white fish, in a crisp light batter. The rounds of crusty fresh bread and garlic mayonnaise don't need ordering. They are assumed.

'What luck.'

'I think it's open every day, though perhaps not Mondays.'

'Where?'

'Here. The boats don't go out on Sundays, do they? So it probably doesn't open on a Monday, most good fish places don't.'

'No. What luck bumping into Rodrigo in the rastro and finding the house.'

'Very funny, but you got us out of it well.'

"'I'm serious, it has great potential.'

'Oh dear. You are serious aren't you?'

Years ago, when trying to explain an idea to a client, Stephen routinely reached into the left inside pocket of his suit jacket for a pen. Unlike the suits, this reflex has never gone and his current uniform of polo shirts don't have pockets; so, nowadays that action kicks in my reflex to reach for my bag where I always keep at least three pens and a scale rule.

Maro was the first but not the last of our houses to begin to be designed on a paper tablecloth. Basically, what we were thinking of buying, and indeed did buy, was a space between two buildings. There was nothing existing that could be saved or was actually worth saving apart from the fireplace in the kitchen and the front door key, a good eight inches of roughly-hammered iron. But the house had potential - I was told.

Within days the deal was done. I'm sorry, if you want to read about the horror stories of buying a property in Spain, then this is not the book for you. The title deeds were in order, both lawyers and vendors turned up on time, and accepting the usual wait of at least two hours at the notario, it all went to plan. That evening we were at a local restaurant and coincidentally the friend of Rodrigo arrived with his wife and her aunts to celebrate the sale. After the meal they invited us to their table for a drink and, as usual, I was expected to sit and talk with the women. During dinner we had been discussing a name for our new house and I asked Maria what her mother's name had been. Carmen de la Valera.

In Granada we ordered a hand-painted plaque from our favourite ceramics factory. It is owned by the Professor of Ceramics at Granada University who is also responsible for replicating tiles in the Alhambra Palace across the gorge from where he works. One of the final jobs for the builders when the house was rebuilt was to cement this plaque into the wall by the front door. To our surprise most of the street arrived to witness the impromptu ceremony. Many of the older ladies who had grown up with Carmen had tears in their eyes. They pointed out the places in the house where, as young friends of Carmen, they had played and been allowed to stay overnight in the one bedroom shared by the whole family, all eight of them. Matilda, the next door neighbour, arrived carrying two bunches of frilly, blood-red carnations. One bunch she gave to me, saying that she wished luck to us and all who stayed in the house. The other bunch she explained, she would take to the church and pray for God's blessing on the house and all who stayed there. Casa de Carmen de La Valera, a very grand name for a very small, but very beautiful little house.

Between buying the house and cementing the plaque, there were six months, a lot of work and a big learning curve. With the theory in mind of 'better the devil you know' we asked Paco, our Frigiliana builder who had done many bits and pieces for us by this stage in both Casa Rosa and Panificadora, if he would be interested in the work. He responded with what we have come to call the Frigiliana Shrug.

THE SHRUG

———

Many years before, holidays in Casa Rosa with Stephen's young children often included taking Irene, Antonio's grandaughter, and Luisa, Mayte's daughter, with us on a trip to the beach. We figured that entertaining four was as easy as, and often easier than, entertaining two. On one of these trips, after lunch at a beach restaurant, we asked them all if they would like an ice cream. We got three 'yes pleases' and a shrug of the shoulders from Irene which we took to be a 'No'. So three ice creams were ordered and eaten. On leaving the beach a few hours later again we offered ices.

'Annie. Ice cream?'
'Please.'
'Ben?'
'Yes.'
'Luisa. Helado?'
'Si. Gracias.'

'Irene?—and before the question was out 'Si Si Si. Por favor. Por Favor. Gracias'

She had, at the grand age of seven learnt very quickly, that foreigners don't easily understand the Frigiliana Shrug.

The shrug is explained by the fact that this area had until thirty years ago been so very poor. Nowadays to be seen not to need anything badly enough to show enthusiasm is a sign that you are not that badly off. This manner of exhibiting pride has been picked up by the children. We also see it in our everyday dealings with tradesmen. Stephen will stop someone in the street and almost beg for the bill for work completed five months before and we get ... The Shrug.

Having been assured by Paco that the work would only take three months and that he could start in the middle of January, we were very relaxed when we signed a contract with our agents to have the house ready for rental by the end of June. Saturday the 28th was a date etched in my brain.

Towards the end of February we were getting seriously worried. Paco was not answering his phone. When we passed him on the road he would wave, smile and accelerate, ignoring our frantic gesturings.

Lourdes and I had got into the habit since that very first day of having a cup of coffee together every morning before she began work. It helped my Spanish, she brightened the day and was always full of the latest gossip from the village.

'You seem sad.'

'No, Lourdes, not sad. Just a little worried about the house in Maro. Paco had promised to start work six weeks ago. We have to have it finished in June.'

'This is a problem for you. Yes?'

'If it is not finished it will be a problem. Yes.'

This was an understatement. By the end of February I think we were both waking up in the middle of the night, Stephen vowing to find and kill Paco the next morning. Me, remembering programmes on English television showing people who had booked their holidays and ended up in a building site. My worst nightmare involved a man named Cook standing with a microphone at our bedside.

Paco arrived that evening with the news that he would be starting work in Maro the following day. Nothing was ever actually said. Lourdes arrived the next day and observed that I appeared happier and that she was glad to see it. Lourdes is an angel without the wings and Paco, like most of the village people, is a relative of hers. I once casually said to Lourdes that it seemed to me that she must be related to at least half of the people in the village, she was appalled, 'Jackie, please, please, far far more than half.'

ON SITE

For Paco and his team of four it was a big step up. They were used to dealing with small building works in and around the village, but they had never rebuilt an entire house. Maro was twenty minutes away before the new road was built, which meant that it was not practical to go back to Frigiliana for meals. As always, they started at eight and stopped at ten for breakfast, a half-hour ritual during which they moved outside to sit in sun or shade, depending on the temperature.

The most junior of the labourers, Jorge, soon arrived back from the local bakery with freshly baked baguettes which were cut open with a penknife, a saw, or just torn apart. Huge, over-ripe tomatoes would be squeezed on to the bread, followed by a tin of tuna or anchovies in olive oil. Jorge, Antonio, Jose and Sebastian washed these 'bocadillos' down with a litre of water each and finished breakfast off with three or four oranges per person. Watching this every morning brought back vivid memories of a greasy spoon cafe two doors away from our office in London. There the windows were always running with condensation and congealed grease. For breakfast or lunch the clientele wanted sausage, double egg, bacon, fried slice, chips,beans and a tea with four sugars. Not many years ago in the UK there was a revolutionary new discovery called the Mediterranean Diet.

Health and Safety are not two words that go comfortably hand in hand with Spain and Building. Before anything could ever be built in Casa del Carmen a lot had to be pulled down. The walls and ceilings were well over a hundred years old and the original mud was pure dust. The masks that Stephen bought were received with a polite nod and, like the hard hats he had bought previously, they then disappeared under a deep layer of exactly what they were supposed to protect from. Jack hammers bounced around noisily an inch or two away from the open-toed sandles worn by their operators, and when scaffolding was required, holes were knocked in the walls, planks were pushed through propped up on poles and secured by old cement sacks.

Work on the little house went well, except that the weather was against us. April that year had many rainy days and builders here do not work in the rain. In fact, they don't work at all on a day that merely begins with rain. Waking up one morning to a downpour, we resigned ourselves to another lost day. But by ten the rain had stopped, the sky cleared and the sun grew strong. We drove to Maro looking forward to seeing a hive of activity. Nothing. No one. Nada.

We went back to the village and spotted the car and motorbikes we recognised so well outside the favourite bar. Inside were our team. Their usual custom of meeting for a coffee and brandy at seven never changes: however, with the weather against them, this custom is prolonged and, by ten in the morning, regardless of the sunshine, it's too late and probably not advisable even to think about asking them to work that day.

By the beginning of June we were really panicking. Paco seemed to think that the deadline of June 28 was when he had to finish his work, despite many conversations to the contrary. Reality was that when his guys finished the whole house still needed a 'builders clean' before furnishing and at least three coats of paint. We tried to get them to finish one room at a time but with a week to go we still had them all over the house.

Once again Lourdes came to the rescue. Despite Spanish machismo, women rule their houses here and this was to be one of Lourdes's new houses. She arrived with HER team, her two sisters and a cousin. No contest. The fiddly little jobs upstairs were finished that day. That, she instructed, left two days for them to finish downstairs before she would be working down there. They were like lambs to the slaughter. Yes, Lourdes, No, Lourdes, Three bags full, Lourdes. It is the only time I have seen a big muscle-bound Spanish builder, carrying a rubber bucket of cement in each hand, tiptoing across the floor and looking behind him in fear of the dusty footprints in his wake.

Friday the 27th of June. The plaque went into the wall, the last of the tiles were laid on the terrace, planters were planted with sweet smelling jasmine, blue and white plumbago and gaudy geraniums, we put the hose pipe into the empty pool mid-afternoon. Amazingly, it all came together. Inside, the bed was installed and made up, pictures were hung, bookshelves filled and the kitchen was stocked with all that was needed.

Relieved, exhausted and very proud of what we had all achieved, we finished inside at about eight that evening, just as the builders finished outside. They didn't know that we had a kitchen fridge full of beer until we pointed them in the right direction and an impromptu party began. It was hot, and the ten twelve packs of San Miguel disappeared faster than the pool was filling, but it didn't stop them. Bigote was first, diving from the steps into no more than three feet of water and the rest were not far behind.

They left just before midnight. We cleaned up and then without a word between us began a tour of the little house, spending four or five minutes in each room remembering when and where we had bought this old door or that old chest, delighting in the end result of the walk- in shower built with more than two thousand tiny hand-made tiles and, finally, agreeing that using the traditional canes between the wooden ceiling beams had been the right decision.

SPANISH POINTERS

When we locked the door behind us at about two in the morning it felt like walking away from a new-born baby. If it was you who rented a house called Casa de Carmen in the village of Maro for two weeks from the 28th of June 1999, please breathe a big sigh of retrospective relief. You don't know how very close you were to have been sharing it with all of us.

PEOPLE ON HOLIDAY

————

It was our habit to meet and greet our clients and show them around our two houses. The agency did what was called a 'Rep's Visit'. This seemed to serve the purpose of confirming that you had arrived at the right place, logged any complaints, sold guided tours and recommended restaurants—the 'don't forget to tell them Angela sent you and they will look after you' sort of thing. Call me cynical, but it is amazing how often you could find Angela and friends eating in one of her 'must try' but actually very average restaurants.

I can now look back and see how naive we were when we began to rent our houses. We had come from the 'customer is always right' school. I still think it is a good school, but it seems that many customers have changed.

Nowadays the compensation culture kicks in fast. For example, we bought some beautiful hand-crafted glasses in a village in the Alpujarras, six of each for wine, water and whisky. They were of recycled glass with a blue tinge. We were equally proud of the dinner and side plates that we ordered from our man in in Granada, a hand-painted set each with a different cheeky little bird in the centre. The letter of complaint had two points. One: the plates didn't match and two: 'it is not possible to drink white wine from blue glass'. Only last week, we had a call to say that a lady staying in Casa Rosa last October had just reported that she had left her jewellery box behind and was making an insurance claim for three thousand pounds! Wouldn't it be nice to have so much jewellery that it takes five months to realise that three thousand pounds worth of the favourite pieces you took on holiday hadn't come back with you. It is the only incident in six years, but we decided a long time ago having heard horror stories from other owners of rented homes that if it ever occured we would stand by our girls. To use a local expression, they are 'as honest as Mary' and over the years have handed us two expensive watches, five pesetas, one hundred and thirty Euros (more money than they make in a month with us), a wallet full of credit cards and a beautiful pair of diamond earings. All of which we have sent, registered post, back to their owners. Not quite true, we kept the five pesetas. We have never once received a note of acknowledgement, let alone a thank you.

Most people however, are fine, and some are delightful. Soon after moving into the Panificadora, I met our Casa Rosa clients in the street. They were an elder-lyish couple from Merseyside.

'Hello, how are you enjoying your holiday?'

'Right good. And thanks for all the food. We didn't expect anything, so I packed a packet of Smash and a tin of Spam.'

'Everything OK in the house?'

'Yup, have'nt had a J Cloth out of me hand since I arrived, it's great.'

I was horrified. 'The house was clean when you arrived, wasn't it?'

'You could have eaten off the floor, and that's the way I intend to keep it, it's right beautiful.'

True to her word, when they left we hardly knew they'd been.

Next came the mistress. I showed an elegant early fifties couple into the house one Saturday evening and invited them to join us for a drink the following lunch-time, as was our practice at the time. Stephen and Peter got on well immediately and walked through to the garden in animated conversation, leaving me with Helen and sorting out drinks.

'White wine would be lovely.'

'And for your husband?'

I wasn't being formal; I just have a lousy memory for names and 'Peter' had evaded me for that moment.

'Peter's not my husband. He has a wife of course and two children, I'm the mistress, have been for over twenty-five years.'

This was actually more information than I wanted to

know. It was not that I could possibly have grounds to be righteous or make judgements about such things, just that I had a feeling that our habit of a quick drink with new arrivals was not going to turn out that way this time. Three hours later we had the full story, wanting it or not. They were both lawyers and I found it vaguely amusing that she was a divorce specialist. Tuesday, Wednesday and Thursday nights they spent together at her flat (bought by him) in Kensington. Weekends she usually spent with friends whilst he went 'home'.

'Christmases cost you a fortune, don't they, darling? He has to be with the family in Shropset, so he flies me to the sun and of course I always have to have a little present from Peter to open, being all on my own on Christmas Day, don't I, darling?' Last Christmas's little present was flashed on a finger that could hardly support it.

JOSE MARIA

Yet another of the joys of living here is that we are able to spend so much more time with Jose Maria. Many years ago, long before we had Casa Rosa, we spent a late June holiday in the little village of Montejaque near Ronda. Ronda has to be one of the most spectacularly sited cities in Spain, perched on a massive rocky outcrop and bisected by a deep limestone gorge. We had rented what turned out to be a very very basic self-catering cottage, the last house on the western edge of the village. We enjoyed many good simple meals in the only one of the three village bars that served food. As usual in these places, mother was in the kitchen, father behind the bar and any children capable of not dropping plates helped out when necessary. In this case the children were two boys of eighteen and fourteen. The eldest, Jose Maria, would serve our meals with style, taking care to lay the plastic table with its paper tablecloth and cheap cutlery as if he were handling fine linen and china. He would then linger in the hope of practising his minimal English. Within the first week we had managed to establish that his aim was to work in England and learn the language, which would give him many more possibilities for a brighter future in Spain. He was saving and hoped to be able to afford to go there within three or four years.

At that time Stephen was working on a big project designing Smithkline Beecham's new London HQ and, as it was nearing completion, recruiting temporary staff to supplement the furniture installation crews. With a rush of blood to our holiday heads, we suggested on our penultimate night that perhaps Jose Maria might like to come and work for us for three months starting that September. He could live with us, earn some money and learn the language. Obviously delighted by the offer, he of course would have to talk to his parents. The following night they greeted us with open arms and tears.

We went home, sent him his ticket, and we found ourselves two months later standing in the arrivals hall at Gatwick airport, wondering what the hell we had done. We needn't have worried.

Spanish waiters make the world's best long-term house guests. Jose worked nights, but we worked long days, often coming home to a Spanish tortilla cooked to his mother Maria's recipe. The secret is… drop the hot cooked, diced potatoes, onion and garlic into the cold whisked raw eggs, stir, then leave them for at least twenty minutes before they hit the pan. Everyone adored him. There was the natural suspicion at first of someone hired by the Managing Director and staying in his house, but Jose was a very hard worker and as eager as a puppy to learn everything. The installation crews worked in pairs and, from the start, Jose was teamed with Ricky, one of the senior guys and an all-round good person. Ricky took him home to sample his wife's cooking and meet the kids, he introduced him to his friends, his favourite pubs and clubs, and taught him to speak West Indian slang. Within a few days, on the rare occasions during the week that we bumped into Jose at home, he would greet us with a hesitant yet perfect 'Hey man, whats going down?'

With Jose in tow we became weekend tourists in London doing the usual touristy things, a boat trip down the Thames to Greenwich, visiting the Tower, the Palace and the Art Galleries. After three months, his English was rather good. As we left for work early in the mornings, he would be arriving home and winding down, usually in front of a video. He was especially fond of a movie called Uncle Buck. By the time Jose left, three days before Christmas, he could recite it word for word, and we had found a friend for life.

The following May we spent the Montejaque village fiesta with Jose and his family. Their bar was open twenty-four hours a day for those five days. Maria proved that it is possible to peel potatoes in your sleep and, as the last of the revellers were thinking of going to bed at six or seven in the morning, the more pious of the villagers arrived for a coffee and annis before the first Mass of the day. When we left at the end of a week, Jose's father, Jacinto (Hyacinth!) presented us with a set of keys to their house, saying that now we would always have a home in Spain.

Two years later, we were back in Ronda, honoured to have been asked to act as witnesses at Jose's wedding to beautiful Ana. The night before the wedding Jose, Ana, Stephen and I spent several hours in the church of Santa Maria la Mayor arranging the flowers and pinning posies of mountain herbs tied with cream ribbons to the ends of each pew. The following day, we were the first people to arrive in the church square, about half an hour before the ceremony was due to start. Had we not been there the night before we would have worried that we were in the wrong place. By ten to two, however, people began to appear, everyone stood outside chatting, but the huge old doors to the church were still firmly shut. Jose, with his parents and brother, arrived on foot on the dot of two and proceeded to mingle with the crowd greeting old friends, talking and laughing. It was another fifteen minutes before the car bearing the bride stopped in front of the still-closed church doors Jose went to the car, helped Ana out and took her hand, together they walked up the old stone steps and Jose lifted the huge brass knocker and let it drop. Immediately a small Jew's Door opened and the priest asked why they were here. My Spanish was just good enough to understand this and I was in a complete panic. We had decorated the church the night before, family had arrived from all over Spain, a reception for two hundred people was only hours away and the priest was asking why they were there.

'We wish to marry.'

'Then enter.'

It is a local tradition, and a rather charming one if you are prepared for it. The doors were flung open, Jose and Ana walked down the aisle hand in hand and sat on the middle two of four chairs placed in front of the altar. Jose's mother and Ana's father sat on either side of them. The general informality of Spanish life, their easy acceptance and tolerance of the needs of every generation, continues around their ceremonies. The fact that the stars of the show got seats should have given us a clue that this was not going to be quick. Parents of young children began emptying sacks of toys into the aisles, the kids settled down to play while friends and relatives settled down to catch up on the year's gossip. Nobody paid any attention to what was happening at the front for at least forty minutes until suddenly it seemed that Jose and Ana had been declared man and wife. Then everyone kissed everyone else. They don't have his and hers sides at a Spanish church wedding, quite the reverse. From the moment you walk into the church behind the couple they see it as two families and groups of friends merging.

For the rest of the day and well into the following morning the party continued and now, years later, I jump everytime the phone rings hoping it is the call to say that we are, once again, godparents.

Whilst in Ronda, Jose suggested that we go to the corrida, the bullfight. Ronda is home to one of the oldest Plaza de Toros in the country, built in the early eighteenth century. Jose proudly told us that it is the dream of every aspiring matador to appear there. Bull fighting is second only to football in Spain as a spectator sport and yet in the newspapers here it is usually reported in the arts section rather than the sports.

I shouldn't even have considered it. I knew I wouldn't like it, but stubbornly I wanted to be able to say that I had formed that opinion from experience, not hearsay. I know, I know, I know. We queued for our tickets and given the option of sol o sombre—sun or shade—chose the more expensive shade. It was to start at five on an early September afternoon. It started well, the three matadors, each to face two bulls, paraded around the ring in their stunning traje de luces (suits of light) beautiful hand-beaded trousers, great bums and cropped jackets that literally sparkled in the early evening sunshine. They were accompanied by their team of banderilleros and picadores. Although I didn't realise it at the time, these are the ones who, on foot and on horseback, stick spears into the poor, not so little things before the matador finally finishes them off. If the matador achieves a clean kill he is awarded one of his victim's ears. If he has been especially brave he also gets the tail. Whoopeee! It was balletic. The men's bravery and skill was breathtaking, but the bot-

JACKIE TODD

tom line is that the minute those bulls enter the ring they don't stand a chance; even if they got lucky and killed the matador they would still be killed anyway. I left after the first bull, arranging to meet Stephen outside later, and achieving what I had set out to achieve: the ability to say from experience that bullfighting is most definitely not for me.

SO HERE WE ARE

So there we were. Three years had flown by. We had three dogs, three cats and three houses. Still not a Spanish pointer or a Mediterranean tabby, but the village had adopted us and it certainly felt like home. English people living here would sometimes ask, 'Do you go home often?' and didn't seem to undertand our response that we went there every day. I was invited to nativity plays, swimming galas and children's birthday parties. Stephen went into the mountains on shooting forays, although he didn't carry a gun.

In early January the thrushes fly down from the mountain pines to eat the olives and the hunters wait until twilight at about six in the evening, then shoot the ready-stuffed birds on their return. In the early forties, at the end of the civil war, Gerald Brennan writes in South of Granada of the eerie stillness of a land without birds. Then people were starving, the birds were all killed and eaten. Today it is more for sport, although the waste-not-want-not culture remains and the few they shoot are taken home, plucked and cooked. It seems like a lot of effort for little reward; a plucked thrush makes a poussin look obese. Around this time Stephen also renewed his love of football, forsaking Liverpool to become a season-ticket holder and passionate supporter of Malaga football club. Social activities here are still very much segregated.

We had permanent suntans. Stephen was a dark mahogany and I was forever nagging him about wearing a cap and using a factor-thirty cream. I was more of a light beige and much more careful. It is yet another sad fact of ageing that most older men look better with a good tan whilst the women look as if they need ironing.

His other new passion was the disease that can render some of the most innocent and educated people capable of almost nothing else. It affects conversation, life style and dress code.

'I had an eight on the fifth today.'

'Well done, darling.'

'You're not listening.'

'Yes, I am. An eight on the fifth, very impressive.'

'It is a par three.'

'Very very well done.'

I try to show enthusiasm - honestly I do—it's just that the game seems so futile. One week Stephen has triumphed at the ninth and the following week it is that same ninth that has ruined not only his score, but his life.

Whilst I indulge my love of gardening and am rewarded with little things growing, Stephen's rewards are often huge ugly cups that sit on the top shelf of our airing cupboard until they are won the following year again, destined for the next airing cupboard—or so I suspect. Occasionally, he will return triumphant with a voucher for a meal for two (excluding wine, to be used on a Tuesday or Thursday) at a restaurant that we would pay not to go to. What finally finished it for me was overhearing a very loud woman dressed head-to-toe in Burberry golf clothes braying to a friend. "Well darling, as I always say, if you can't play... DIS. PLAY."

JUST AN IDEA

In our third year, I began spending one morning a week helping out at the Taller De La Amistad, a workshop for mentally handicapped young people. It had been started five years earlier by an amazing lady whose own son is handicapped, though compared to many of her subsequent charges, only mildly so. Here, when a child is born with any form of impairment the family close ranks, and every member is expected to pull their weight in the added burden of keeping a child more or less behind closed doors. From listening to Gloria, the lady who started the workshop, these children are usually very well treated, often indeed, thoroughly spoiled, but just not allowed to be part of what we call normal society.

Her vision was to integrate these youngsters into the local community. By providing the resources to create a workshop, they could, with encouragement and help, produce saleable items, thereby becoming more valued members of their community. Here, certainly amongst the older generation, what you contribute within your capability, not what you do or what you earn, is still of the greatest importance. Gloria works tirelessly, not only with the youngsters but also at creating fundraising events for the whole scheme. She badgers the town hall and local businesses for support and sponsorship and charms all the local performers into giving their acts for free.

It was at a Christmas fundraising dinner for the workshop in the smartest hotel on this stretch of the coast that Stephen did it again. He came up with a seemingly casual thought that was to change our lives for the next few months.

We had taken a table for ten and, knowing that there was to be flamenco singing and sevillana dancing as part of the after dinner entertainment, we invited Lourdes, Charo and their husbands to join us. Charo, Lourdes' older sister's sister-in-law began working with us when we needed a cleaner for Casa del Carmen and I still enjoy the Saturday cleaning rota that starts 'Charo in Maro and Rosa in Rosa'.

Watching the show, I was more entertained by Lourdes than by the acts themselves. She was both mesmerized and animated: her top half rigid, with chin propped up by hands, elbows on the table and mouth open. Like a swan, all the work was going on below the surface: beneath the tablecloth her feet, squashed into strappy, outrageously high heels, were tapping and twisting.

'Just look at Lourdes. She's loving it.'

'We thought she would.'

'Just imagine if she lived in London? If this is her reaction to this, can you imagine what she would be like seeing a West End show?'

'Take her.'

'What?'

'Take her.'

'To London?'

'Yes.'

'Take Lourdes to London, to see a show?'

'Yes It's just an idea, but you haven't been back for almost three years. Do some shopping, visit friends and take Lourdes with you for company and to see a West End show. It would be fun.'

'Are you having an affair?'

'Yes. With a very attractive goat. So go to London for a few days, leave me in peace, go. Go and have some fun.'

The coffees and brandies arrived at our table. I wasn't sure how or when to suggest that Lourdes may like to come to London with me, but something told me that it was a suggestion better made in public and here we were. If she went home and days later told Julio of the offer then I felt that the whole thing would never get off the ground.

'Lourdes, you enjoyed the show?'

'It was the best I have ever seen. The dancers were fabulous, the singer had such a great voice, true? No? And the guitarist, he is my younger sister's husband's cousin. I had heard that he was very good but I have never seen him play before.'

'In London there are many theatres with shows, certainly as good, possibly sometimes even better than this, performing every night.'

'Every night?'

'Yes. At least twenty different shows all within an area the size of the village. Stephen has an idea. He has just suggested that you and I should go to London for a couple of days and see a show. He will pay for it as a birthday present for me. What do you think?'

Charo started clapping and laughing, 'Go, Lourdes, Go.'

Lourdes laughed, smiled, looked at Julio, then laughed again, shaking her head. His face was unreadable. She turned to us.

'Me. I go to London. London, England. I have never spent one night away from the village in my life. It is not possible. It is beyond my dreams.'

'OK, forget it. It was just an idea.'

Again she looked at Julio. He is a man of few words. He leant forward slowly and placed his not inconsiderable forearms on the table. We all held our breath.

'Thank you. Thank you very much, it is a most kind offer. Lourdes would love to go to London.'

Everyone at the table cheered.

UNA PREGUNTA
—A QUESTION

We booked the flights for late May. By the end of January the whole village knew that Lourdes was going to London. Every time she arrived, she had a new question.

'Jackie. Una pregunta.'

'Yes, Lourdes? '

'Will I need a passport? Someone said that I would.'

Stupidly, I was only just beginning to realize what a really big deal this was going to be for her. Of course she needed a passport and of course, never having spent a night outside of Frigiliana, she had never needed one before.

'Stephen. Una pregunta.'

'Yes, Lourdes.'

'My father says that it is dangerous to fly and that

we would be much safer driving to London, and that it would be quicker too.'

'Don't worry, Lourdes, it will be much quicker and much safer to fly, especially with Jackie's driving. Trust me.'

'Una pregunta. My father says that when we fly we will be nearly as high as the clouds.'

'Lourdes, when you fly, you will be much higher than the clouds, you will be able to look down on them.'

Crossing herself, she made Stephen promise that he wouldn't repeat this to her father or she would never be allowed to go. The questions continued for four months, what should she pack, how much money did she need, would she be able to speak to her family whilst she was away, should she bring her own food. Excitable at the best of times, the tensions were rising and she was totally impossible in the final week before we left.

LOURDES
GOES TO LONDON

On that sunny Tuesday morning in late May we collected Lourdes from the village. All of her family and many of her friends had turned up to wave her off. She, her mother, grandmother, and both her sisters were crying and clinging to each other. I began to think that we had made a mistake. She had borrowed a suitcase from us at least two months before saying that she wanted to start packing early and be sure that she didn't forget anything. Judging by the weight of it she certainly hadn't.

Sitting in the back of the car on the way to the airport she was uncharacteristically quiet, not surprising though, considering the trip to Malaga was a huge event in itself. Then, after about half an hour:

'Jackie, did you find it difficult to have to cook eleven different meals all at once?'

'Eleven meals? What do you mean Lourdes?'

'Lunch and supper for today and we won't be back till late on Friday so I cooked eleven meals. Carmina is going to serve the suppers and my mother and Aurora are doing the breakfasts and lunches between them.'

'Shut up, Lourdes.'

I had felt, until then, that I had more than fulfilled my housewifely duty by leaving a casserole in the fridge for that night and ample sandwich fillings, after which he was on his own.

Malaga now has a sizeable airport with an impressive new departures hall, the first of the many things that over the next few days were going to take Lourdes' breath away. She cried again when Stephen left us in the queue to check-in.

'Lourdes, this is supposed to be a happy time, it's an adventure.'

'I have never been so happy in my life.'

More crying.

Normally I would say that the flight was uneventful. It was, but that was me seeing it through the eyes of a pretty seasoned traveller. This time though, it was a joy to experience it through new eyes, those of a first timer and that was indeed the beauty of the whole three days that Lourdes and I spent in London. We were flying with Iberia, the Spanish National airline, which both eased and complicated things as all signs and instructions were always first, and often only in Spanish.

'Jackie, why do we need life jackets? Jackie, why do

we need oxygen masks? Jackie, what are life jackets and oxygen masks?'

Usually a calm passenger, I was beginning to ask myself the same questions.

I think Lourdes was the only person on that plane who was glued to the safety briefing as we taxied to the runway, to the point of undoing her seatbelt, not an easy feat, and getting up to look behind her at the rear exits as they were pointed out. She sat in the window seat and squeaked and squaked all the way to London.

Heathrow. As if travelling with a child, I was in charge of tickets and passports and it was here that I began to realize the extent to which Spanish camposinos have a respect, yet a mistrust and fear of officialdom.

'My passport is new. Will that be a problem?'

'No, don't worry.'

I have never had one before. Will that be a problem?'"

'No problem.'

'My picture is not very good. Julio says it looks more like my mother. Will that be a problem?'

We sailed through customs, picked up our bags - 'we stand still here and our bags will come to us, they will find us?'—luckily they did, and I pushed the always defiant baggage trolley towards the taxi rank. This involved meeting Lourdes's next new experience, the revolving door. Heathrow's huge revolving doors, designed to get as many people as possible, together with said trolleys, through quickly. In the middle of these contraptions are glass windows displaying the latest, no longer duty free, perfume and jewellery promotions. Lourdes was mesmerized. Concentrating on steering, it was a few minutes before I realized that she had done at least six circuits. On her next lap, I reached in and fished her out.

The driver of the black cab that took us into central London was as friendly and chatty as I fondly remembered most London cabbies to be.

'What lingo's that then?'

'Sorry?'

'Language love, what are you two speaking?'

'Oh, Spanish.'

'Thought I recognized it, I've been to Malta on me holidays.'

Surprise, surprise, it was raining. The new 'fast lane' on the M4 was a wonderful regulation as we were in a taxi. Though I am sure that had I still been in the company car and therefore destined for the other two lanes, I would have been cursing like hell.

As it was, we sailed into town.

'Julio would love it here. It's so green, his goats would be so very happy.'

Lourdes had borrowed a camera from a friend, a simple point and snap that would feature largely on this trip. Seven hours in, we already had photos of us leaving the village, photos of Malaga Airport, the plane through the window of the departure lounge, and of the baggage hall at Heathrow. Now Lourdes would not let the taxi driver go until he had posed with her whilst I snapped. He was charming and seemed almost flattered by the request—maybe he had done the same in Malta.

It was early evening, about seven-thirty. We checked into the hotel and, leaving Lourdes in her room with instructions on how to lock the door, not to open it to anyone and to call me if she had any problems, I promised to be back in an hour. That evening we were going to meet John, a good friend of ours whom Lourdes had met several times in Spain. John and I had agreed the week before that we would meet outside the Odeon in Leicester Square and go for a meal in Chinatown.

Knock Knock. 'Lourdes, it's me.'

'How do I know?'

'How do you know what?'

'That it's you? You told me not to open the door to anyone.'

'Yes but this is ME Lourdes, ME who told you not to open the door, so open the door

OK, please just open the door.'

Inside it quickly became clear why her suitcase had been so heavy. In the space of that hour, in addition to hanging up her few clothes, she had turned her room into a shrine. There were three statues of Jesus, four of local saints, including Sebastian and Antonio, many crosses, two sets of rosary beads—good Catholics always carry a spare—and pictures of all her family.

In front of the Odeon in Leicester Square had

seemed like a very easy and traditional place to meet. What neither John nor I had known at the time, was that it was the opening night, the London Premiere, of the latest Bond movie. Traffic was backed down Piccadilly, we got out of the taxi half-way, paying and apologizing to the cabbie who grunted and did a swift U-turn.

London instincts, hibernating for three years, quickly kicked in. Knowing that we were very late, I grabbed Lourdes' hand and pulled and pushed us through the crowds. There were more lights, traffic and people in and around Piccadilly Circus than at any Andalucian village gathering, and here, all of them were strangers. Lourdes was like a rabbit caught in the headlights; she was terrified.

Chinatown. The idea had been to expose her to as many new experiences as possible in only three days. That was all arranged before we left, before I had even begun to understand that most of the things I took for granted were going to be new experiences for her anyway. Not speaking the language, the scale of London, the height of its buildings, the pace of city life. The list was already almost endless and we had only been gone for ten hours.

She was brilliant. She greeted John with such enthusiasm, a familiar face, very welcome at that stage, and then sat with her mouth open as the usual range of Chinese food arrived. Crispy duck with pancakes rolled and eaten with fingers were a big hit and the chopsticks caused hilarity. Her approach was to take one in each hand and use them as spears. It was successful with the deep fried prawns but failed miserably with the seaweed. The laughter coming from our table drew the waitresses who were enchanted. I still can't quite put my finger on it, but there are now so many times that I have watched Lourdes work her innocent magic. People love her. The Chinese girls gave her chopstick lessons. After a memorable meal, we decided to walk down to Trafalgar Square. It would be easier to find a taxi there and the lion statues, fountains and Nelson would be Lourdes' last sightseeing hit and photo opportunity of the night. We were both tired.

'Please, please wait. For you.'

Our waitress was running after us down the street with a pair of chopsticks and a pretty little blue and white china bowl. She smiled, bowed, and gently presented them to Lourdes, who kissed her heartily on both cheeks. It all seemed so natural, good and kind. Words that I had stopped associating with London living in my last few years there.

TIME TO SHOP

‾‾‾‾‾‾‾‾

Eight-thirty next morning, very late for Lourdes and rather early for me, we sat in the breakfast room. I was translating the quite extensive menu and she was trying to get her brain around the fact that you sat down to a breakfast that was delivered to the table, although her husband and son had mastered that one years ago.

'Dos zumos de naranja, dos cafés con leche, y tostadas para dos tambien. Por favor.'

'Vale, algo mas?'

'Nada, gracias.'

It took several seconds after the young girl had walked away for my early morning brain to register that we were in a London hotel, that I had just ordered our breakfast in Spanish, and that, hopefully, I had been understood. She returned with our juices and we established that she was a language student from Galicia working breakfast shifts at the hotel. For Lourdes, it was reassuring, comforting, a bit of almost home.

We walked in the rain through the north of Hyde Park towards Marble Arch. Shopping in England after a three-year absence, it seemed to make sense to hit Marks and Spencer's first for the basics, after which we could have some fun. It was still early and there were what I had sadly become so used to many years before, people sleeping in doorways. I saw them out of the corner of my eye but then resurrected my London tunnel vision and continued walking. Lourdes stopped.

'Jackie. There is a young man asleep here.'

'Yes, Lourdes. Come on let's go.'

'But why is he sleeping here?'

'Probably because he has nowhere else to go.'

'But London is rich. It is a rich city.'

'Yes. That is why poorer people come here.'

'Without their family? Where are his family? Why don't THEY look after him?'

I have always enjoyed M & S's Marble Arch store. I know they have had a bad press, but for me their bog standard stuff is fine and just occasionally they comes up trumps (As you can tell, I'm never going to be a fashion writer.) Lourdes loves to shop in the village's one and only clothes shop or at the clothes stall at the weekly street market, but this was all her birthdays and Christmases arriving at once. When I was a busy working woman, the food hall was a godsend for mid-week supper parties with tarted-up dishes. Add a few fresh mushrooms, a bit of parsley and casually pretend that you threw it together yourself in the copious spare time you manage to organize between doing deals, learning a new language and taking yoga classes. It was also useful to be able to buy basic clothes in a lunch hour, try them on at leisure at home and, if necessary, return them without hassle. In fact, I don't think I had ever seen the inside of their changing-rooms. This was about to change.

Almost two hours later, having tried on their whole spring collection, in every colour, Lourdes bought a skirt. We moved on to accessories. Lourdes loves hats and, coming up to wedding season, the place was full of them She was particularly taken with a huge pink straw top hat, similar in shape and size to that worn by the Mad Hatter in Alice in Wonderland.

'Lourdes you look wonderful. I must have a photo.'

She posed, hands on hips, and at the last minute stuck her tongue out. Click. We both giggled like teenagers. I popped the camera back in my bag and had begun to move on when there was a hard tap on my shoulder. Behind me was a dragon with flaring nostrils dressed in a M & S uniform with a badge saying supervisor—no name—just supervisor, pinned to her impressively large chest.

'I've called security.'

'Excuse me?'

'It is forbidden to take photographs within the store. There is a sign.'

'Oh, sorry, I must have missed it.'

'Well, you will be watched and if you try to take

any more photographs we will be forced to ask you to leave.'

I was two seconds away from letting rip, but then saw the look on Lourdes face, total confusion and worry. She didn't understand a word but she certainly understood the tone.

We turned and left the shop.

'Why was she angry? What did I do wrong?'

'Nothing. You, we, did absolutely nothing wrong, forget it, don't worry.'

A minute later we were in Selfridge's and it didn't take her long to forget. Her first escalator took a bit of getting used to. Stupidly, seeing that she was apprehensive, I stepped on to show her how it was done, by which time I was committed. Seeing me disappearing before her eyes she took a big breath and jumped with both feet.

We worked from the top down. Every good shopper has a plan. The designer clothes floor had prices that left Lourdes awe-struck, with snooty assistants to match. The toy department had electric cars for children that were worth more than most of the old Seats in the village and stuffed toys bigger than any of her husband's goats. Finally the ground floor perfumery. It had not changed, still an assault course of pretty, overly made up young and not so young things trying to spray you as you pass. Instead of the purposeful stride and tight polite shake of the head that I had perfected over the years, Lourdes stopped as soon as anyone approached her. She smiled and pushed her wrists forward to try perfumes, the backs of her hands for lipsticks or eye shadow colours. She eagerly climbed onto a little stool in full view of everyone to have her eyelashes curled and happily allowed her chipped nail varnish to be removed from two nails and repainted so that the girl from Estee Lauder could let her 'experience' a new shade. We were in there for over an hour; obviously she didn't understand a word that was being preached about the lifting benefits of this or the tightening results of that; in fact, she didn't buy a single thing, yet we walked out with enough free samples to keep her and her sisters in cosmetics for a year.

How does she do it?

A brief moment of total panic I'd lost her. I left the shop through swing doors whilst Lourdes chose to resume her affair with the revolving ones. Only two circuits this time though - she was learning fast, but, what if I had actually lost her? She wouldn't even know the name of our hotel. We went for a coffee and I resisted the strong temptation to tie a baggage label to her in Paddington Bear Fashion.

'Lourdes, we must make a plan for what to do if we lose sight of each other. London is much bigger and busier than Frigiliana.' A look of panic swept her face, I went on quickly.

'It won't happen, of course, but better to be safe. Yes? Good. If you can't find me, stand still, don't move and I will find you. Take this card; it has the name and address of our hotel. If I haven't found you after half an hour, give the card to a taxi driver. They are all along here, look, big black cars with yellow lights at the front. He will take you back there and I will come and find you, OK?'

On we went. Debenhams, John Lewis, BHS and every little shop between the major stores, to Oxford Circus. A right turn into Regent's Street. Liberty, Burberry, Aquascutum, but only serious window shopping at Mappin & Webb.

For lunch we met up with a group of my girlfriends, three of whom had already met Lourdes in Spain, and she greeted them like long lost friends. I was almost jealous. Not true, I was really, really jealous. They made much more of a fuss of her than of me and they all gave her little presents. As we tucked into our genuine Italian pizzas cooked in a genuine Italian pizza oven, it occurred to me that the three meals we had eaten since arriving—Chinese, Continental breakfast and now the pizza—were in fact typical English food.

The afternoon, what was left of it, we spent in the new Waterstone's in Piccadilly, armed with a list of at least twenty 'must buy' books for Stephen. It was the days before we had discovered the joys of Amazon. com. and a lack of good English language bookshops in our part of Spain was one of the few things we could find to moan about.

New experience number four hundred and six: The London Underground. Earlier when we had walked passed a tube station, I had tried to explain the concept to her but I don't think that she actually believed

me. We descended into the dirty, smelly, hostile en-
vironment that I was lucky enough to have forgotten
still existed.

It was almost five and the rush hours were beginning. A busker was sitting, crossed-legged, in one of the
spaces at the bottom of the escalator that Lourdes had
this time tackled with mounting confidence, though
still using the two-feet-first-and-jump approach. Always enchanted by music, she stopped dead in her
tracks at the bottom. This time I was behind her—I
was learning too. The resultant pile-up and muttered
curses sailed over her head. There are advantages to
not being able to speak the language. She could not
be moved on, so I manouvred her into a corner and
let her enjoy the music. When the song was finished
she rushed over, stood in front of the bemused young
man so obviously used to being ignored, and clapped
loudly. With a final 'Ole' she returned to me without
having put any money in his guitar case but when I
glanced guiltily behind as we walked on, he was sitting there grinning after us.

Westbound on the Central Line, always shoulder
to shoulder and often face to face, but never eye to
eye with total strangers. For someone with an English
vocabulary of maximum thirty words, Lourdes sure
knew how to use them, albeit in total innocence.

'Hello.'

The business-suited man hanging by one hand from
the overhead rail, reading a quartered Evening Standard recoiled and turned away. Until she had uttered

that simple word, she had been fated to stand with her nose in his armpit, although probably not a problem for someone accustomed to three hundred goats. The woman on her other side got the same greeting. Lourdes got the same response. She looked at me, shrugged and smiled, not having a clue that on her first tube journey, without any pointy elbows or aggression, she had managed to achieve what the regular commuters have been after for years—a bit of space.

That evening, Wednesday, was to be dinner with Julia, our old Spanish teacher, or rather our Spanish teacher of old. It served the dual purpose of meeting up with a good friend whilst giving Lourdes a chance to speak in her own language. When planning this short trip it quickly became clear that it would be impossible to find the time to see everyone that I would have liked, without intruding on the most important aspect of all, letting Lourdes see London. So I combined two reunions with friends who had never met. Weeks before, Julia had insisted that whilst in London, we must come to dinner and see her new flat. Clive, a long term friend and colleague, had made the same offer, having just moved to Twickenham. Knowing who was by far the best cook, I accepted Julia's offer and asked if Clive could come too.

There was also a sub-plot here. Julia was at the time going through a 'what is the meaning of life thingy' and had left her boyfriend of twelve years. Clive had just been dumped by the latest love of his life. Stephen could see what I had in mind.

'It won't work.'

'What won't work?'

'Clive and Julia. Not in a million years.'

'Don't know what you are talking about. It's just dinner.'

'I know you and your scheming and I'm telling you it won't work.'

It worked in a way. The mere thought of a relationship with Clive, probably one of London's most eligible bachelors but just not her type, probably speeded up her return to Moyses. So, clouds and silver linings anyway. Regardless of the very obvious lack of potential romance, it was still a lovely evening. We got back to the hotel in one piece despite Lourdes's piercing scream that made the taxi driver swerve dramatically. She saw a train, her first train, ever, so she screamed, very loudly. Seemed reasonable to me.

DAY TRIPPERS

————

Breakfast. Day two. The same waitress.

'Hello, Lourdes, how are you? Would you like the same as yesterday, and what about your friend?' Lourdes asked me if I wanted the same as yesterday, a question that I had fully understood. How the tables had turned within twenty-four hours.

'Please, yes, we will both have the same. How was college yesterday? '

They chatted for at least five minutes. The girl from Galicia and the 'girl' from Andalucia - in a London hotel.

The previous morning, walking to the shops, we had been accosted in the most charming way by several guides for the many open top double-decker tour buses that trawl the city. This had never happened to me in the twenty years I had lived in London. How then after only four years in Spain had I come to look like a tourist? Or was it Lourdes?

SPANISH POINTERS

We joined the bus at the Bayswater stop nearest the hotel, having bought 'hopper' tickets that allowed us to jump on and off any bus at any point throughout the day. First in the queue, we raced up the stairs and sat at the front, plugging in the headphones and selecting the right languages, or at least trying to. Understanding that we could get off, go see things, then catch the next bus, Lourdes at first wanted to get off at every stop. I pointed out that our plane left at two the next day and therefore this would not be possible. We became more selective. We 'hopped' at the Houses of Parliament. She was enchanted by Big Ben, having seen it on news reports on Spanish television, but couldn't believe how big it was. At twenty to eleven, I bought outrageously overpriced tasteless coffee from a stall on Westminster Bridge and we sat at Churchill's feet in Parliament Square waiting for the chimes. To this day, whenever our newspaper has a picture of Big Ben we save it for her. She has started a scrap book. More hopping for the Tower of London, St Paul's and then Harrods and Harvey Nicks for additional retail therapy. Finally we left the tour at Buckingham Palace, by which time Lourdes knew far more about the history of London than I did. In all of the six buses that we had used, not one had an English soundtrack that worked. Her statements such as 'interesting about the little boy in the Great Fire' or 'fancy that happening in the Tower' were totally lost on me.

Lunch was a sandwich at a Pret-A-Manger. Sitting

on stools in the window, I was thoroughly enjoying the view of London life through her new eyes.

'People walk and eat.'

'Of course.'

'But they walk and eat all at the same time, and talk too, with a phone in their other hand, and they don't look at each other, or say hello. It is as if the people around them do not exist. When is siesta?'

'There isn't one.'

'No siesta? No sleep of the key?'

This is a very old fashioned expression. It comes from the time when after lunch the man of the house, still sitting at the table, would rest his head in his arms with the big old door key, much like the one we inherited from Maro, clenched in his fist. When the key dropped and woke him, it was time to go back to the fields.

Next was Covent Garden to see the street performers and shop in the covered market.

This was a great hit. Market shopping was something Lourdes understood and she picked up several little gifts for her family. Lourdes loves any form of entertainment and there was a particularly good selection in the piazza that day. A limbo dancer, a fire eater that drew squeaks of excitement from her. There was a girl with a pet monkey dressed in Victorian costume offering to let you pose with it for photos, at a price of course. Lourdes was so enchanted by the little creature that against my principles I paid and snapped. To this day it is one of her favourite photos of the trip.

The definite favourite though, was the human statue. At first she would not be believe it was a real man, painted top to toe in silver. He was very good, so good in fact, that I was almost beginning to wonder myself, when suddenly, he reached for his three-cornered hat, doffed it with a flourish and immediately resumed his pose. Lourdes had to have a closer look. She marched up to him and stood on tiptoe with her face no more than a foot from his and her fists tucked into her hips. For a good minute he didn't flinch, then he winked at her, she screamed, the crowd laughed and Lourdes ran and hid behind me.

We sat in the weak but welcome sunshine, me with a glass of wine, and she as always with water and we watched the world go by.

'So many people. There are more people here, in this square now, than live in my pueblo. No one will ever believe all that I have seen.'

'Yes they will, and anyway, we will have the photos to prove it.'

Drinks at six with yet more people familiar to Lourdes. In fact it was no more than three weeks since Paul and Judy had been staying with us. Judy, as always, immaculate in Armani, was already at the Opera House Bar when we arrived, and Paul appeared soon after. Unflappable Judy has a crisis management company and is her own best PR, nothing seems to throw her. If oil spilled from any of my tankers (her speciality) I would call Judy.

The champagne was on ice and, with a nod of Judy's

beautifully coiffed head, a plate of giant prawns piled on a bed of ice were delivered to the table. Prawns were the perfect choice of course, something that didn't faze Lourdes at all; she rolled up her sleeves and peeled twenty to our two. We had just over an hour together before it was time to make for the theatre.

Goodbyes, like hellos, are not things to be rushed in Spanish. Lourdes bestowed blessings on both of them, their families, their health and their wishes for the future. She promised that she would go to church next week to ask for their swift return to Spain. I thought calling Easy Jet would probably have better results, but kept that to myself and just translated.

THE SHOW

'Take Lourdes to see a West End Show' was how the idea for this trip had begun. When the seeds of the idea became saplings, Which Show? became a serious point of discussion.

Predictably, Stephen with his logical mind and economy of vocabulary, after a twenty-four hour gap, came up with the answer.

'Cats.'

'What have they done now?. If it's the new flower bed again, I swear I'll kill them.'

'Cats. It obvious.'

'I can't see them. Where?'

'CATS. The musical. Lourdes won't be able to understand a play. You need to take her to see something that doesn't need words, and she loves animals. Book for CATS.'

The theatre had been home to the show for many years. Once you saw the stage set it was no surprise that it rarely travelled. The foyer, however, was the

typical red plush affair. I bought the programme, the
T shirt, and ordered our drinks, wine and water for
the interval. The bell rang and we entered the audito-
rium.

The story is set in a rubbish dump with the audience in the middle of it. To get to our seats we had
to navigate five-foot long sardine cans and cornflakes
packets. On stage there was the rusty bonnet of an
old car wreck, a sofa with its stuffing spewing out and
a pile of builder's rubble that made me feel quite at
home.

Lourdes was very quiet. We sat in row three, Lourdes
in the aisle, with me to her right.

'What do you think, Lourdes?'

'Jackie, Charo and I would do very well here. I think
they need a cleaner.'

I opened my mouth to respond but was saved in the
nick of time as the theatre lights dimmed.

It was a magical performance. From the opening
bars of the first song we were both enchanted. The
cats were dressed in skin-tight leotards painted to
look like real markings, we had ginger toms, black
and white moggies and even my favourite Mediterranean tabby. They arrived on stage from all over the
theatre, crawling on all fours up the aisles, even ab-
seiling down from the balconies, stopping en route
to brush up against members of the audience. Across
the aisle from Lourdes was a city type with his wife
and children. A cat started to rub itself against his leg,
he sat there, staring straight ahead, obviously rigid

with embarrassment, poor man. The next cat to enter through our aisle targeted Lourdes, who was delighted. She stroked its head and rubbed under its chin all the while exclaiming loudly

'Mi Gato, Mi Gato, Jackie, mira mi gato tan bonito.'

My cat, my cat, Jackie, look at my beautiful cat.

Next came a beautiful tortoiseshell that headed straight for us. Lourdes went through the same performance and then, in heavily accented English, came out with one of her few English phrases and I don't know who was more surprised, me, or the cat.

'Roll over, tickle tummy.'

I saw a second of confusion in the dancer's eyes, then a smile, then a flip, she was on her back with all four 'legs' in the air and Lourdes was tickling her tummy. Lourdes had learnt the expression when Stephen's son, Ben, was teaching Domingo to do exactly that trick to a click of the fingers. I had never thought that she would find the opportunity to use it, especially in a London theatre. During the next enchanting hour we had four more visits, one of the cats even sat on her lap and, ignoring her giggles, proceeded to extend a back leg and wash itself.

Like most good times it was over too quickly; there was a well deserved standing ovation following two encores. As we were preparing to leave, six of the dancers ran to the front of the stage and, as one, pointed long, slim elegant arms at Lourdes, clapped and blew kisses. She leapt to her feet and returned both affections.

What a wonderful day. We walked south, back through Covent Garden. Eleven o'clock and all the theatres were emptying. It was rush hour in show land, taxis were hard to find. When we reached the Strand, I decided that the junction with The Aldwych was probably our best bet. Standing on that corner, I explained to Lourdes that it might take a while to find a cab. Having spent more time in taxis in the last forty-eight hours than she ever had in her life, she was quite happy to wait and just watch the world go by.

A young man approached and waved a cigarette at us, wordlessly asking for a light. I smoke. I have managed to give up the patches and the chewing gum, but not the fags. My only rule is that I don't smoke in the street. Ever. My conversation with Lourdes was, of course, in Spanish, and having overheard it, he probably thought he was dealing with a couple of vulnerable tourists.

'Sorry, I don't have a lighter.'

My response to his request, in unaccented English, obviously threw him for a moment, but not for long. He took two steps back, smiled, then proceeded to light his cigarette from matches produced from his pocket. He stood there staring at us. I didn't like it, it smelt like trouble. Lourdes picked up on the tension.

'Lourdes, let's walk. There don't seem to be any taxis coming up here.'

We walked, quickly, arm in arm. He followed, too closely behind and within seconds was joined by another man.

'Buy us a drink, girls.'

Ignoring him seemed to make him angry. He tapped me on the shoulder from behind, then again, but much harder. The Strand was still busy, but I was beginning to get scared. Suddenly they were both in front of us, they stopped, forcing us to do the same.

'Give us your money, just hand over your bags. Right now.'

It wasn't worth getting hurt or ruining our break that was for sure, but by then I was as angry as I was scared. Over their shoulders I could see the two door-men from the Savoy Hotel, flagging down taxis, no more than ten yards ahead. Clutching Lourdes close and hard, I pushed past and almost frog-marched her into the hotel entrance. The two men stayed on the street, one of them calling out obscenities. We were safe, but, had we actually been two innocent Spanish tourists, I'm not at all sure that we would have been.

So soon, it was time to leave and for Lourdes leaving meant many more long goodbyes. Goodbye to the receptionists, the door man, the porter, the girl from Galicia serving breakfasts. Goodbye to the Phillipino cleaning lady who certainly wouldn't have too much to do in Lourdes' room. When I went to collect her the shrine had been repacked, the bed was stripped, the used linen and towels folded neatly and placed on a chair and she was lamenting the fact that she couldn't find any bleach to clean her bathroom.

We left our luggage with reception and set off for our final couple of hours in the city.

It was raining yet again. On day one I had cautioned Lourdes against buying the first things she saw as presents for her family, consequently, we now had to retrace many of our steps to pick up the 'must have' items. So again we were close to Piccadilly when I remembered my promise to an old friend in the village to bring back her favourite breakfast tea from Fortnum's, their own blend.

In hindsight, I suppose explaining this to Lourdes didn't really prepare her for Fortnum & Mason's food hall. As ever it could have been a stage set—though certainly not from Cats—everything was presented so beautifully. The theme of that moment was peacocks. In the center of every display were stuffed birds, either with tails dropped and spread, or fanned like rainbows above their heads.

'Jackie, this is a shop? Yes?'

'Yes, Lourdes. I'm buying some tea for Marta.'

'This is a shop? A food shop? So can you buy these birds to eat?'

'No, they are only for decoration, they are dead and stuffed just like the heads of the mountain goats and boar in the village bar.'

'How sad that we cannot take a photograph, I would love to show my family what food shops look like in London.'

OK. I was cheating a bit. Fortnum & Mason's food hall is not exactly your average Spar or even Sainsbury's, but the idea that Lourdes could have a photo of this and explain to her village that it was a London food shop amused me enormously. I went over to one of the many assistants all dressed in pinstriped trousers and frock coats.

'Excuse me.'

'Madam?'

'Would there be any problem if I took a photograph of my friend in front of one of the displays? It is her first time in London, and she would like a photo.'

'Madam, Fortnum's would be honored. May I suggest, if you would permit me to use your camera, I could take one of you both.'

Learn a lesson M & S!

The taxi driver that we hailed in Piccadilly was delighted to learn that we wanted to go to Heathrow via our hotel in Lancaster Gate. It was the middle of the day, the traffic was heavy, much better to get out of town, it was a good fare. He talked non-stop. When Lourdes asked me if I knew all the taxi drivers in London I was stumped. I didn't know any, then I realized that in Spain, the land where everyone talks to one another, taxi drivers are the exception. They don't talk, they just drive, very, very fast. In England, certainly in London, it is usually the reverse.

Heathrow, and with amazing luck we managed to find that very same trolley and weaved an unsteady course to the Iberia check-in desk. I presented the tickets, the passports and prepared myself for the usual questions.

'Is this your baggage?'

'Yes.'

'Did you pack it yourself?'

'Yes.'

The usual, but for Lourdes it was official and therefore important. I was standing there nodding and shaking at the right moments and idly wondering that if I were a suicide bomber, would I behave or answer any differently? Then came the big question.

'Are you carrying anything for anyone else?'

'Yes many, many things.'

I snapped out of my stupor.

'NO. Lourdes NO. You are not carrying anything for anyone else.'

The check-in girl raised a pencilled-in eyebrow.

'But I am Jackie, I am. Remember, for my mother I bought a cardigan, the one with the pearl buttons, I wanted it in blue, her favourite colour, but they didn't have her size so I bought the green, but still I think she will like it. For my father a shirt, I hope he will like that, it is always so difficult to know what to get him. It was difficult to decide what to get for my sisters too, there was so much choice, but in the end, remember, they both have scarves and tea towels.'

She turned back to the girl behind the desk. 'Carmina's has a picture of the Big Bin, the clock and Aurora's has the Queen's horses in her corral. Aurora's three children have toys, no that's not true for Eva, in the end, I bought a hair slide, she is ten and now too old for toys, and for Aurora's husband....'

She gave a three or four minute monologue, the queue behind was backing up impatiently and yet the check-in girl was enchanted and seemed suddenly to be in no hurry. It was established that Lydia was from Asturias and had never been to Andalucia although her parents had visited friends there. That Lourdes had never been to Asturias and didn't even know anyone who had. Finally, we got our boarding cards. With a delay and therefore over two hours wait in the departure lounge, Lourdes and her charisma reaped yet more freebies, this time mainly miniatures of whiskey and brandies - shame she doesn't drink.

At the boarding gate we were asked to stand aside for a moment, then told that we had been upgraded to Club Class. It could only have been the work of Lydia. I was delighted, it meant more space and free Cava all the way home. Lourdes, whose charm, I was sure, had achieved this upgrade, was totally oblivious.

An onlooker at Malaga airport that evening would have been forgiven for thinking that Lourdes was meeting her long-lost husband and had her friend in tow. She launched herself at Stephen from a distance of at least three feet. Having applied a serious layer of one of her sample lipsticks in the Ladies whilst we waited for our luggage, by the time I caught up, he looked stunned and rouged.

'Lourdes. Did you enjoy London?'

'Stephen. I do not have the words to tell you everything that I have seen.'

She found the words, millions of them, and with a stunning memory for detail. Although our flight had been delayed, when we arrived in the village just after midnight, all her family and friends were waiting in the street outside of her house. It was as if time had stood still. There were many tears of joy from the women and blessings for her safe return. Her father enquired about what it had been like to be so near to the clouds; at this Lourdes just looked over her shoulder, smiled and winked at us.

It's Oh! so nice to go travelling, but Oh! so nice to come home, or words to that effect and how true. Stephen indulged my euphoria.

'You've lost weight.'

'I don't think so.'

'The dogs have forgotten me.'

'Of course they haven't.'

'It's much hotter than when I left.'

'That was three days ago.'

'Not making sense am I?'

'Not really.'

" It's just so good to be home."

SEVILLANA:
DANCES AND DRESSES

By the time we got back from London, Feria, the annual Festival of San Antonio, was less than a month away. For the previous two years I had watched enviously as the village women and men that by then we knew so well swirled around each other in the beautiful, four-part dance called Sevillana. It originates from the time when, at festivals, the girls approaching marriageable age, normally kept securely behind the rejas - the ornate iron-barred windows of their houses - would be allowed to attend dances during fiestas. Watched, especially by their families, but also by the whole village, these courting couples would dance as close to each other as possible, but were never allowed to touch. The result is a dance far steamier than anything seen in today's discos.

Stuffed into a prickly pink tutu at the age of three

by an over-ambitious mother, I then, with little talent, endured tap, ballet, ballroom and Latin American lessons. It is therefore really rather surprising that I still love dancing, but I do.

So, when Lourdes had suggested, the previous February, that I join the Sevillana class starting that week in the village hall, I jumped at the chance. She would come with me, she said. It was a long time since she had learnt and the practice would do her good.

Bless her, she was born to dance and certainly didn't need the practice, but I was the only foreigner in a class of twenty and very grateful for her company and support.

Remember the rub your tummy and pat your head at the same time trick? This is Sevillana. To begin with there is a lot more intricate foot work than in classical English dance, but it doesn't stop there. After the first lesson I felt quite proud of my grasp of things, after the second, positively cocky, but then came the arms; 'Reach up to pick an apple, eat it and throw it away.'

'What?'

Whilst your feet are doing Fred Astaire proud, you also have to produce creative windmills with your arms. The action is likened to reaching out to pick an apple from a tree, pulling it towards you to eat, and then, with an underarm backward movement, throwing away the core. By the end of lesson twelve and the fourth and final part of the dance, the feet were doing quite well but the arms still had a long way to go. Lourdes was touchingly pleased with my progress and pronounced that I was ready to dance at that year's fiesta.

About ten days before Fiesta week, the flamenco dresses arrive from Seville at Encarnation's shop in the village. She normally sells between ten and twenty dresses a year, but each one is tried on by at least fifty village women who have no intention of buying. It is just part of the ritual and excitement in the build-up to the event and accepted as such. The dresses are deceptively heavy and cleverly designed to be altered with ease. The inside seams have a good three inches of excess material, allowing a size twelve to become a ten or a fourteen with a little needlework.

I arranged to meet Lourdes at seven one evening outside the village's clothes shop. Outside was a good idea. Inside were thirty or more women, teenage girls and children in varying states of undress.

These dresses are perfect for the Spanish figure which, in general, tends to be small on top and, there is no way to put this politely, enormous around the bum. They cling down to the waist or just below and then flare and ruffle, hiding a multitude of sins and cellulite. The bodices are tightly fitted and the backs dive almost to the waist, therefore wearing a bra, at least one that you could buy around here, is out of the question.

When my turn came, at least an hour later, I chose two dresses, almost second-hand by that stage, and headed towards the changing cubicle. Lourdes and her sisters came with me, each carrying two dresses apiece, though for them, there was no intention of buying. In the space of the average toilet cubicle, the four of us stripped to our knickers and wriggled into yards of heavy frills.

I had spotted the dress that I wanted the moment I arrived in front of the shop, a deep rich blue, almost navy, with red, white and tiny yellow flowers embroidered on the three layers of frills. At the time it was on a dummy in the window—but not for long. It was the perfect length but far too tight on top and far too big around the hips, I was more than a little disappointed and about to take it off when, Lourdes took over. From behind me she reached into the front of the dress and without ceremony repositioned my boobs, the left more left and higher, the same on the right. She called for Encarnation's mother the seamstress, Concepcion. Of course the name has a different, more religious meaning here, but I do still have a problem with the idea of calling your baby daughter after the biological process that preceded her arrival. Through a mouth full of pins, Concepcion declared to the whole shop that it was the first time in her sixty-five years that she had been required to let a dress OUT at the top and take it IN at the bottom, they all came to look and I felt like the star attraction at the freak show, but when she had finished it fitted perfectly, and the past pleasures of my Armani business suits or my Aquascutum cashmere coat paled in comparison.

At that year's feria, I danced till I dropped.

TIN TIN

―――――――――

'How was the golf?'

Silly question really. By the time he had carelessly parked the car, slammed the boot, slung the clubs into the basement and stomped up the steps, even the dogs knew the answer to that one. After very brief, single wags of low slung tailed greetings, Charly, Domingo and Niña made a wise and swift retreat to their baskets, heads down. Time to change the subject.

'Remember the dog I told you about? It has been around on and off for at least a few weeks now. The one that looks like the dog in the Tin Tin cartoons. What was the name of that dog in the Tin Tin cartoons? Well, anyway, today it was back again and it looks worse than ever, really sad and thin. It has no road sense, cars have been swerving to avoid it. But it won't last long out there.'

'We have more than enough dogs.'

'Of course we do. I wasn't suggesting that we take it in.'

'Good.'

Because of the heat, rubbish collection is pretty efficient around here. There are wheelie bins at the edge of every cluster of houses which are emptied every night.

Ours was three minutes' walk away, up past Antonio's bar; Stephen made a nightly pilgrimage. That night, standing at the kitchen sink, looking out of the window, with my very poor long distance sight, it seemed to me that Stephen was bringing the rubbish back again. He was definitely carrying something white.

'It's the Tin Tin dog I've been telling you about. Where did you find him?'

'Lying under the rubbish bins. He is so, so thin, almost starved, and he can't stop shivering, even in this heat. I couldn't just leave him out there.'

'No, Of course you couldn't. But Stephen, we don't need any more dogs.'

I just couldn't resist the chance to turn the verbal tables.

By this stage we were relatively practised in the art of introducing a new animal to the pack. Stephen sat on the floor in the corner inside our front door with the Tin Tin dog in his arms and the other three came and had a good sniff until they were satisfied that there was no threat. In this case we felt that it was especially important that he was introduced to the others gently. He was in such a poor way; pitifully thin, almost bald, he was terrified of everything and

Stephen had the slightly soggy trousers to prove it. We need not have worried. It was immediately obvious to our three that this excuse for a dog couldn't fight its way out of a paper bag.

Yet more radio appeals and vet visits. In Rafael's waiting room the following day, Stephen spotted a fresh cut on the dog's front leg that had been stitched. Rafael said that he hadn't stitched it, he would have certainly remembered such a strange-looking animal. A tour of the town's veterinary practices gave us the answer. His name was Loopy. The Danish vet had stitched him several times recently when he had been brought in by various strangers who had clipped him with their cars. He gave us the mobile phone number for his German owner and Stephen made the call.

'Hello, I believe we have found your dog. White with huge black ears. Loopy?'

'It iss not my daug. I do not vaunt zee daug. Go zee my ex-husband. Nomber 10 Camino Viejo.' The line went dead.

We went to Number 10 every day for the next two weeks but there was never anyone there. The note we had pushed under the gate was gone, but we had not had a call, and meanwhile we were both becoming very attached to Loopy, or Tin Tin, as we called him.

He had more or less stopped trembling when we got close to him and was very subservient with the other three dogs, rolling on his back, avoiding eye contact and curling his tail under him whenever they approached. For the first week he ate and slept, ate and slept, then he slept, curled into a tight ball, and ate. As he began to relax, we nicknamed him Flat Pack. He was so thin and white that when lying on his side, he looked like an IKEA bookcase or wardrobe waiting to be assembled.

Back to Camino Viejo for what must have been the twentieth visit and this time a thin man in his early thirties with long mousy greasy hair answered the door. It was early afternoon, but we had obviously woken him.

'Hello. I believe we have your dog, white with huge black ears. Loopy? Look we have him here, now, in our car.'

'It iss not my dog. It belongs to my ex-vife.'

'Yes. Well, actually, we have spoken to her and she says that she doesn't want him, she says that he is yours.'

'In zat case, I spose you muss bring it in.

Stephen and I took one look at each other and then, without a word between us yet in unison, 'We'll keep him. If you really don't want him, that is.'

'Gutt. Zank you. Guttbye.'

When he slammed the door in our face without a second glance at Tin Tin, without enquiring about our ability to care for him, we knew we had done the right thing. After all, we had three dogs, one more wouldn't make much difference Or so we tried to convince ourselves.

In the first six months he didn't put on much weight, in truth he never really has. The hollows between his ribs have filled out a little, and from being almost bald, his wiry coat has grown thick and shiny. Best of all, he now looks us in the eye, wags his tail with such joy as to swipe two coffee cups to the floor and falls asleep on his back with all four legs in the air. It is amusing to us that so many of our English visitors enquire about the breeds of our brood. There seems to be an obsession with pedigree which in my opinion is responsible for many of the Bride of Frankenstein animals that the Kennel Club seem to promote and prize so dearly.

Of Tin Tin, many people say lurcher, then pause, and add that it could be a very, very hairy greyhound. White with bat like black ears and a big black patch on his bum, the rims to his eyes are pink. Until his fur grew, with his spotted skin, he looked like a very thin, bald Dalmatian. If I were to choose an actor to play him in a movie, it would have to be Donald Sutherland in his role in Kelly's Heroes, and I have been very tempted to buy him the leather flying-helmet. We have already decided that Elizabeth Hurley gets the part of Niña. She would like to be a good actress and would look great in a black dress held together by safety pins, Niña that is. The jury is still out on the other two, although Charlton Heston is on the short list for Charly's role, and Micky Rooney would have done a good Domingo.

A month or so later we were sitting in companionable silence on the terrace late one evening staring up at a clear starry sky with the four dogs at our feet, when Stephen did it again.

'Snowy.'

'You have got to be joking. It's August, and anyway even in winter it has never got anywhere near freezing point here for over thirty years.'

'Snowy. The dog in the Tin Tin cartoons. It was called Snowy.'

DO YOU PLAY GOLF TOO?

August, the month of madness. Everything is full, the hotels, the shops the restaurants and the beaches. Many tourists drop what was a dubious dress code to begin with and wander around the town sporting speedos, beer bellies and bum bags. Last summer I gave thanks that at least the man walking towards me was wearing a white singlet, until, up closer, I realized that that must have been yesterday; he was naked from the waist up and seriously sun-burnt. The queue at the bank's Foreign Exchange counter stretched out of the door, even longer than usual. Eventually the woman at the head of the queue turned to the people behind her and announced in a very loud voice, 'I don't, know what all the fuss is about. Just because when they asked me at home where I was going and I said France, they went and gave me the wrong travellers' cheques. Now, here, they are making a big fuss about it.'

One reason to be thankful for the Euro!

Michael, my hairdresser, called one morning to ask if any of our houses were empty. In August? Silly question, Michael. He went on to explain that the man having his hair cut at that moment had arrived in Nerja the night before with his wife and daughter. That they were here for four days to look at the possibility of designing a golf course and the only flight out of Dublin at short notice had been a cheap package. They had taken it assuming that they could move to a better hotel or rent a villa when they arrived. In August! I knew where they were staying and felt sorry for them. I promised to make some calls and get back to him within a few minutes, which I did, but only to report that as I had expected, everywhere I could possibly think of was full. I was about to put the phone down when something funny came over me. To this day I don't know why I did what I did.

When we had first talked seriously about living in Spain, we had discussed creating an exclusive bed and breakfast place. It was only a thought and a daft one at that, luckily quickly dismissed. Stephen likes his privacy and I hate cooking breakfast before midday, so not exactly the right credentials.

'Michael, if they are really stuck, I suppose we could put them up on a sort of bed and breakfast basis. I've never done it before, and we have four dogs now, that might be a problem, especially with a child. Ask him, and do explain that I have never done this before. If he is interested, he can come up and have a look, then decide.'

'I'm giving him directions, they will be with you in twenty minutes. '

Christie and the two Annes, his wife and nineteen year old daughter, arrived and introduced themselves. As charming as only the Irish can be, they pronounced the bedrooms and bathrooms perfect, had no problem with the fact that I was new to this sort of thing, said they only ever had coffee and toast for breakfast anyway and fell instantly in love with the dogs. They went back to the coast to pack and were installed within the hour, with instructions to make themselves at home. They had a swim and we all sat on the terrace with a bottle of icy white wine.

'Michael said that you were here to look at the possibility of designing a new golf course. Do you play too?'

'I have been known to.'

'That's where Stephen is now, playing golf. He only took it up a few months ago and is really hooked. He should be back any minute.'

I heard the car pull up and went to explain our new state. It didn't seem fair to let him just walk in on strangers.

'Darling, how was the golf? Ummm, we have people staying with us.'

'People?'

'Only for three nights. '

'People. For three nights.'

I explained Michael's phone call and my rather less explicable reaction to it.

'They are very nice. He is here to look at designing a golf course. You'll find that interesting, won't you? Anyway come and meet them. The wife and daughter are both called Anne and he is Christie something, Connor I think.'

'Christie? Irish? Here to look at designing a golf course?'

'Yes.'

'Christie O'Connor?'

'I think so, Yes.'

'Christie O'Connor Junior.'

'No, no. He doesn't look very junior.'

'Do you know who Christie O'Connor is? His shot basically won the '89 Ryder Cup, playing with Canizares, a two iron if I remember rightly, to within four or five feet of the pin, people still talk about it.'

'Well, I'm sure he's not the same one, but they are very nice and he did say that he played some golf.'

He was the same one. They stayed with us for three nights, one of which we spent in Antonio's bar. Antonio was on particularly good form, clapping the hollow-handed clap of the local cante jondo, with the accompaniment from Aurelio of a slow beat of his walking stick. Christie picked up two spoons and joined them. They were both delighted to learn a new form of peasant folk music. At three in the morning I pointed out it was getting late and got the Irish response that 'the man who made time made plenty of it'. I translated for Antonio and discovered that the Spanish have exactly the same expression. They also touch wood and avoid walking under ladders, though Friday the thirteenth holds no fear; it is Tuesday the thirteenth that you have to watch out for here.

'I wouldn't be minding nine holes in the morning, it would be doing me arm good.

Would you be interested?'

Stephen went pale. He had been playing for less than for a year and had a handicap of about one hundred and eighty. Gamely, he agreed, thoroughly enjoyed their half round and Christie taught him a lot. When they left, promising to return soon, Stephen asked me if I had charged them for they stay.

'Of course, that was the agreement.'

'Don't you realize that I would have paid ten times that just to have met, let alone have had a game, with Christie O'Connor.'

Golfers.

CASA CAROLINA

——————

About a third of the way through the project in Maro, Juan, our lawyer, had called to ask if we would be interested in buying a house about half a mile from us. He acted for the elderly English owners who were finding it too much for them. Having lived there every winter for thirty years, they wanted a quick, quiet, no fuss sale. Our first Antonio, now a friend, has one of the town's largest estate agencies. He bemoans the fact that when it rains and the tourists can't hit the beaches, many of them hit the agents. They occupy their day viewing houses with little or no intention of buying. This was exactly what these people were trying to avoid.

We agreed, with little enthusiasm, to have a look at the house and arranged to meet Juan there later that morning, though the work in Maro was going full steam and we both felt that we had enough on our plates at the time.

The house was exactly what you would expect from

an elderly couple after thirty years of habitation. Much too much furniture and clutter, lots of dark brown heavily varnished wood, beige walls and pink upholstery. Like the owners themselves, it was looking rather tired. The price they were asking was more than fair and reflected the fact that they didn't have a pool, although the large garden, their pride and joy, was stunning. We made the usual polite comments and 'we will think about it' noises and left. Ten minutes later Juan was at our door offering the house at a reduced price with the typically Spanish explanation that 'they likes you'.

Still we said 'no' and forgot about it for more than a month. At least I forgot about it.

'We should have gone for it you know. We were stupid.'

'Gone for what?'

'That house. Casa Carolina. It wouldn't have taken a lot to change it around, new floors and doors, paint everything white and we would have had to put in a pool, of course. Then, if we moved the entrance so that people arrived from the little lane below and walked up through the gardens past all the fruit trees, which would be rather lovely, we could have shut the existing approach off and still have more than enough land to build another house."

Even to me this was an intriguing proposition. An empty plot where we could design from scratch, another adventure. Parcelas, building plots, in that area were selling for almost as much as they were asking for the house. We agreed that the following morning Stephen would call on Juan to see if it was still on the market, though we doubted it very much. Early next morning, before Stephen left for town, Juan phoned us again with his final, final offer. We bit his hand off.

We had brazenly and obviously fallen in love with Casa Rosa and then with the Panificadora and paid the asking price for both. It just goes to prove that not being interested can be the best form of negotiation, though that was not, in this case, our original intention.

SURPRISE, SURPRISE

Lourdes' birthday is on the twenty-first of July. Every year we now have a 'women and children only' pool party. The first of these, six years ago, was a surprise.

She had left at two on Tuesday, saying that she would see us on Friday if not before. It was only later that afternoon I realized that Friday was her birthday. I called her sisters and we made plans. The joy of July, like May, June, August and September, is that you can almost guarantee that the weather will be fine and outdoor eating can be planned in advance.

She arrived on Friday wearing her usual smile and lycra and we chatted over our coffee cups, yet she appeared a little quiet. I knew that she was disappointed that I had forgotten her birthday, but that she was determined not to mention it. I busied myself in the kitchen, cooking two huge paellas, laying out plates of jamon and chorizo, preparing salads, roasting peppers and making pizzas for the children. She walked onto the terrace as I was stacking plates and I explained that friends were coming to lunch.

She would finish as usual at two and, as arranged, her sisters, her son and her best friends, together with their children, began to arrive just before. It was difficult to smuggle nine women, three heavily pregnant, and fourteen children into the kitchen without attracting her attention but with much giggling and shushing we managed it.

'Lourdes, would you come here for a moment, please.'

The double doors to the kitchen were shut. I pointed in their direction with a nervous look and explained that there was a funny noise in there. In little more than a year she had become used to my over-reaction to the birds, mice, occasionally rats, gigantic geckos and huge spiders that come into the house and are part of day-to-day life. Rolling up her sleeves, she pushed the doors open with an air of authority, prepared to take on whatever it was. But not prepared for what she encountered.

'Cumpleanos Feliz.'

'Happy Birthday to you.'

It took us all at least five minutes to stop her crying. We had a wonderful afternoon. The children turned into happy prunes after many hours in the pool and my Spanish vocabulary increased richly, surrounded by the local gossip.

Since then the party has grown. The three 'bumps' that bounced around the pool that first year, all now have little brothers or sisters. Last year it was sixteen women, only one with a bump; Carmina, Lourdes' little sister was finally pregnant. And twenty- three children. On these occasions, Stephen is always packed off to our cortijo, much to his relief. He takes the dogs, his favourite sandwiches, a good book and a golf club. Standing on the crest of our land with a big bag of old golf balls beside him he hits them into the valley below. This serves two purposes; he assures me it helps to improve his swing, and the dogs have great fun and exercise chasing after the balls, though they very rarely bring them back. As one of our dog books advised, if you want a dog that retrieves—buy a Retriever—and for all the varied genes that our lot must possess, I don't think there is one retriever gene amongst them.

BACK TO WORK

―――――――

The full heat of the summer was fading. It was time to look seriously at getting Casa Carolina ready for the following year. Replace the tired terrazzo floors with terracotta tiles. Strip all that dark and heavily varnished woodwork and paint it white - a sentence that takes seconds to write, but days of nail and back-breaking work to achieve. Change the heavy doors to the half-glazed variety to double the amount of light entering the house. Retile both bathrooms; those Barbie pinks had to go. Where to put the pool? The garden was large and mature. Wherever we dug it would, sadly, mean losing at least two prime trees. For a week we went there every day at different times. With oranges and a flask of fresh coffee for breakfast at 7.30 in the morning, a time that Stephen found especially productive because I didn't speak. Lunch times with sandwiches, evenings with a bottle of wine. It was a luxury to be able to do this before making any major decisions and has paid great dividends. The pool and summer-house that we built are in exactly the right place to take maximum advantage of the long hours of sunshine that bless the garden, with views to sea and mountains that are spectacular.

With the house we also inherited another Antonio. The seventy three year old Antonio de dos dientes. Dientes are teeth and he is the proud owner of two in a fetching shade of saffron yellow, one at the top, one at the bottom, though inconveniently, they are on opposite sides of his mouth. Like many of the older men in the village, he has an accent as thick as treacle. I understand roughly one word in four. He has been Carolina's gardener for more than thirty-five years, it is his second home. He knows every plant, every tree, every stone.

We have been told that when we bought the house he feared he would lose his job.

It wasn't the loss of income that worried him, he was paid for only four hours a week but spent, and still spends, more than four hours a day there, it was the idea that it may no longer be his garden. Stephen has promised him that he will have the job for as long as he wants it and that he can be buried there if he chooses, a suggestion which delights him and I truly hope he doesn't hold us to.

THE CORTIJO

―――――――

Whilst we were finishing work on Carolina, Paco, our builder, always keen to do the odd deal on the side, asked Stephen to go and look at a plot of land that his friend was selling. It was about twenty minutes drive above the village. He thought Stephen might find it interesting. Stephen did. We had been watching the incredibly rapid increase in the price of property and land around here and we were pretty sure that if we could buy the right place at the right price, just sit on it for a few years, then sell on, we would be improving our returns. Thirteen thousand square metres of land with a small cortijo, a cottage. It has piped water from a well, rumoured to have never run dry, but no electricity. We call it the world's most expensive private picnic site because that, so far, is all we have ever really used it for.

We go there and let the dogs run; it is very rare that a car goes past. Only three or four minutes drive down a dirt track off the only road that rises from Frigiliana and although less than half an hour from home, it is considerably higher than where we live and therefore, in summer, much cooler. The lack of electricity is actually a bonus. As the daylight fades we light candles and enjoy the mood that only candle light can provide. It has already provided the site for some of the best days of my life, sitting picnicking with friends in our overgrown meadows, full of wild flowers and trees laden with figs, lemons, olives and pomegranates. Looking down on the gleaming white village dwarfed by the mountains, The Sierras (The Saws) that tower jaggedly above it, and watching the Trans-African ferries on the distant Mediterranean horizon.

That winter, on one of the lost days between Christmas and Los Reyes, the sun was bright though the air was cool. We wrapped up, relatively speaking, in long trousers and fleeces, and along with the turkey and stuffing sandwiches we packed our books, our four dogs and a bottle of wine into the car and spent a peaceful afternoon at the cortijo enjoying just that, together with the views. Driving home as the sun was disappearing, we slowed to allow the last few goats of the herd to cross the road in front of us and looked out for Julio. We are used to seeing them around. Julio, Lourdes's husband, has his corral only fifteen minutes away from our cortijo and we always put a bottle of beer in the cool box alongside our wine for when we meet him in the mountains.

This day, however, it was Julio Pequeno (Little Julio, the son) who was walking the herd. He was throwing stones, trying to contain three hundred dumb (and goats make sheep look bright) animals, whilst one of their number was in the process of giving birth by the side of the road. He was kneeling beside it.

'Hola, Julio. Can we help.'

'Hola, Stephen. Yes, please, she is a first time mother and not doing that well. The baby has started early.'

With a calm wisdom and experience well beyond his fourteen years he took charge.

The mum-to-be was lying on her side, bleating furiously.

'Hold her tight under the forelegs as tight as you can with both arms. Just don't let go, and keep your face away, she is normally very sweet but right now she may bite.'

I was standing at the 'working end' and could see that both back legs had already arrived.

Julio took the two tiny legs in one hand and put his other on the mother's stomach. He waited calmly for two or three minutes, then as it contracted he pulled very smoothly and gently and one of the first goats of the new millennium spewed into view.

'It's a boy.'

Within seconds the mother was on her feet. After biting through the cord, she started to walk away. It was an impressive recovery but more than a little short on bonding. We both stood, feeling useless, until Julio threw a rope at Stephen and told him to keep the mother there. He sat with the newborn in his lap and, putting his face to its mouth, sucked and spat three times. Grabbing the reluctant mother, he used considerable force, a sort of rugby tackle, to lay her on her side and kneaded a teat until it produced milk. Bright kid, it caught on straight away and began guzzling greedily, but within a couple of minutes the mother had again had enough. She stood up, shook the baby off the teat and walked towards the rest of the herd without a backward glance.

'Stephen, would you mind taking the new one back to the corral? My grandfather is there. He will look after it. We have to be out for at least another hour, I could carry it, but he would be better in the warm.'

'What about the mother?'

'Oh she's fine. She will walk with us.'

I was incensed. No wonder she was so pissed off. Where were the champagne, the bouquets of flowers, the phone calls, the telegrams, the presents and the visitors? When was she going to have her warm aromatherapy bath and change into her new, carefully chosen nightie ready to hold court and look serene? After all she had just been through—she got to go for a walk.

I wrapped the baby in Stephen's favourite cashmere jumper which had been lying on the back seat, something he has never quite forgiven me for, although the stains did come out eventually. We drove to the corral and handed him over to abuelo (grandfather) and therein lies another story.

The previous Spring a wart had appeared on the middle finger of my left hand. I never had been warty;

it was my first and I hated it. It sat on the next finger to the beautiful emerald and diamond ring that Stephen had given me many years before. It grew rapidly, was soon competing with the diamonds and despite every remedy that was recommended, including something called 'Bazooka' sent from England, it looked like it was there to stay. When this thing was in its infancy, Lourdes casually mentioned that I should go and see her father-in-law, who was famous in the village for getting rid of warts. According to her, he only had to touch someone and the wart was gone. By this time it was competing with the Leaning Tower of Piza. I was almost desperate enough to chase a bit of witch-craft, but I didn't need to. Within two days of handing the new- born kid over to Lourdes' father-in-law, just as one would pass a small baby, the hated wart had halved in size. Within a week it had disappeared, and when I told Lourdes about it she simply replied, 'Of course.'

JAVIER AND ROSARIO

W e were just finishing our meal at Las Chinas, a popular restaurant in the village, where Sebastian serves a fish soup rivaling anything you could find in France. At the next table a couple with a sleeping baby had arrived after us. As is usual here, and a custom we find charming, before sitting down they had nodded and wished us 'buen probecho' enjoy your meal.

With the timing that only small babies can perfect, as their plates were put in front of them, she woke and began to cry. She was not to be ignored. Both mother and father tried to humour and jolly her on shoulders and laps whilst their food began to go cold and she just got louder and louder.

I offered to take her and let them enjoy their meal, though it is most certainly a suggestion I would no longer make in England. They passed her over with a smile, I somehow managed to calm her, and they finished their meal in peace. That was our first meeting with Javier, Rosario and their exquisite baby daughter, Claudia. Although we had never met them, they, like ninety percent of the village, knew who we were, where we lived and that I had taken Lourdes to London. It turned out that Rosario, until becoming pregnant, had been the cleaner in Casa Carolina for many years. I asked if she knew Antonio, the gardener; she knew him rather well actually, he was her father. It was a delight to be able to so easily understand Javier's clear unaccented Spanish. Born and brought up in Barcelona, though married to a village girl, to me he sounded like a newsreader. With hospitality typical of Andalucia, they enquired whether we would join them at their house for dinner the following week. Over time they have become our best friends in the village and we are now proud godparents to Claudia and her little brother, Nicolas, one of the three bumps at Lourdes's party.

FIESTA FIESTA

Tradition dictates that the end of a building project is marked by a fiesta. Finishing work on Carolina heralded our third. The catering, as always, was easy. Plates of thinly sliced air-dried hams, rounds of goats cheese, huge salads and about forty sticks of bread. The cooking on these occasions is men's work: kid stew in an industrial-sized pan, with a sauce of ground almonds, pine nuts, onions, garlic and the local wine, simmered over an open fire.

The only thing that differed this time was that when, as usual, we offered to provide the meat ready for cooking, Paco accepted. It was, we thought, a sign of acceptance that finally, after three years, we were being trusted with such an important task. We arranged with Lourdes that Julio would have two of the poor little things ready for Stephen to pick up when he took her back to the village the following day. They were skinned and hanging in her shed, about four months old and roughly the same size as Niña.

'Lourdes, they need carving up.'

'Yes, tell Jackie that first she must... ahhh Jackie.'

'If I go home with these... like this, I will be as dead as they are.'

'Yes, I was forgetting, but I think you are right.'

They spent an hour and a half on her kitchen floor butchering the kid. Stephen came back looking slightly pale and carrying two big bin liners which he tried to 'hide' in the fridge. That evening Paco and Bigote arrived early to start the cooking. At our previous two fiestas we had eaten the M & S food hall version of kid stew. It had always arrived pre-cooked and just had to be heated on the barbarcue. This time we were starting from scratch.

Sitting on the steps of the terrace, Antonio Bigote had both hands working away inside one of the black bags.

'Antonio, what are you doing?'

'Jackie, you don't want to know.'

'I do, Antonio.'

'Jackie, you don't want to know.'

'I do, Antonio.'

'I am cutting the tongues and eyes out of the heads.'

'You were right Antonio, I didn't want to know that.'

Men arrived: this was a builder's fiesta. As the woman of the house I was there of course, and in fact my eighty-year old mother and her lifelong friend, Brenda, a mere chicken of seventy-seven, were here on holiday. But it was not in general a 'bring your loved one' sort of occasion. Years later at our next fiesta we turned this idea on its head with hilarious results.

Paco, as head builder, had now assumed the role of head chef.

'Jackie, would you get the jug I put in your fridge when I arrived?'

'Here, Paco. What is in it?'

'Jackie, you don't want to know.'

'I do, Paco.'

'Jackie, you don't want to now.'

'I do, Paco.'

'OK. It's the blood that was drained from the animals when their throats were cut, it makes the sauce rich and thick.'

'You were right, Paco, I didn't want to know that.'

He smiled. We ate at midnight, the goat stew was pronounced excellent and when I found Paco and Bigote huddled in a corner looking secretive I should have known better.

'What are you two doing?'

'Jackie, you don't want to know.'

'I do.'

'Jackie, you don't want to know.'

'I do.'

'"We are eating the brains. They are the best bits.'

They were right of course, I didn't want to know. It was a great night, hot and still and the cicadas joined the party, competing with the men to see who could make more noise. The perfume from the honeysuckle and summer jasmine was at its peak; there was a full moon reflected in the swimming pool. Mum and Brenda proved themselves impressively good at the rumba and passable at a passadoble.

Paco's younger brother—if you think Antonio Banderas is cute then you would seriously fall for Jose Antonio - is the local policeman and was on duty that night. At about two in the morning he arrived in uniform driving the Jeep with POLICIA LOCAL in huge letters on the side. He parked it on the steep track at the side of our house and jumped over the wall to avoid being seen. The 'one beer' turned into more than several and four hours later he left as he had arrived. Jumping over the wall, saying that he would let the car roll back down the hill and then turn the lights on when he reached the road so as not to attract attention. Two minutes later he rolled the jeep down the track, but instead of flicking the switch for the headlights, he hit the siren by mistake and woke the whole village.

BAMBOLEO

—————

July the sixteenth is the day of Carmen; the fisherman's saint. As the sun dips, her statues are taken from the churches to the beaches all along the coast. They are then put on to fishing boats for a trip to sea to pray for the safety of her men and for good catches in the coming year. The older local people wouldn't dream of swimming in the sea before this day of blessing, despite temperatures in the eighties. They wait each year until the sea has been blessed and cleansed. Every available craft follows Carmen in this procession. The fishing fleet from each port is scrubbed squeaky clean, their rigging covered in flags and bunting, their horns tooting. Each boat carries about a hundred family and friends. At the other end of the scale are the tiny inflatables with outboard motors carrying two or three brave teenagers bobbing around alarmingly in the wake of the larger boats. We were invited by neighbours to join them on their small sailing boat, moored at Caleta, for the evening of Carmen and we eagerly accepted.

Caleta de Velez does not make its living as a harbour for yachts. Marina Del Este, just half an hour East of Nerja, is the closest to a luxury harbour that we have around here. It has the required art gallery, designer clothes shops and over priced restaurants, whereas Caleta is very much a working port about twenty minutes drive back along the coast towards Malaga. At six every morning, except for Mondays, the fish are auctioned by the crate-load. We have only managed to get there for the auction once in all our time here, as I don't really do six a.m. any more. Some of the last boats to come back were still circling just outside the harbour walls, sorting their catches and throwing guts overboard, to the delight of the swarming squawking seagulls.

Inside the cavernous shed that is the market, men still in oilskins stood over their catches doing their deals with the suited businessmen wearing Wellingtons, wielding calculators and mobile phones. The contrast in cultures was striking.

Most of the contents of the crates were still squirming, several crabs were half way across the floor with an obviously pre-planned escape route, and the smell was pungent. Large articulated, refrigerated lorries sat by the dock with their engines running, waiting for the deals to be done and to be on their way to Malaga, Seville and even to Madrid. The Spanish people pride themselves on the freshness of their fish. Lourdes wouldn't dream of buying a clam unless it was still sticking its tongue out at her.

On the night of Carmen, we arrived at the port at seven and lurched on board, greeted our fellow guests and set off back towards Nerja. The journey that had just taken us twenty minutes in the car was reversed on water and took over two hours. To begin with the sails were up in an optimistic yet futile attempt to catch the few puffs of warm air that could not even be called a breeze. Whilst the sails were up, flexibility was essential.

Booms or whatever you call the things that swing the sails around were booming.

Years of yoga are to be recommended when you are suddenly commanded to raise your feet, duck your head, and twist to the right. Admitting defeat, the outboard engine was coaxed to life and we chugged along very enjoyably. With a beer in hand and the sun setting, it was a most welcome respite from the land-locked heat of the day. For us it was also the first chance to see from the sea the coastline which we knew so well, giving it a completely different depth and perspective.

We arrived off the Balcon de Europa at nine. A rocky promontary jutting out to sea and approached, landside, by a wide avenue of eighty-foot palm trees, the Balcon is the social centre of the town. Every Sunday evening the town's people dress in their finest and take the air. The children are scrubbed and polished, the girls with satin bows in their hair matching those on the backs of their smocked dresses. Little boys wear junior suits with ties and waistcoats and you have to hunt to find the small babies amongst the lacy frills of their prams. It is also the place where the tourists photograph each other, eat ice cream and pay too much for a coffee or a beer and, these days, where many street performers ply their trades.

You can have your portrait painted, your cards read, your hair beaded and braided. You can listen to the South American group playing pan pipes or just stand watching the beautiful young couple who dance superb sexy tango.

That night, however, we were in the privileged position of looking up at the packed crowds on the Balcon from our space on the sea. Carmen was delivered to the shore on the men's shoulders, reverently installed in the honored boat and set off on her annual tour of the coast. As the light faded, a tiny motor boat hired by the town hall did its rounds, throwing flares into the sea and handing out long tapers to all the 'boat people'. To torchlight and shouts of 'Viva, Viva, Guapa, Guapa, Carmen, Viva', we arrived back in front of the Balcon for the firework display. We had heard several people rave about how good the fireworks were. Our host reversed the boat a little further away from the Balcon and scooped up two big buckets of sea water to have at hand just in case. We sat watching with anticipation. What appeared to be a small rocket was fired from the little beach below the Balcon. Trailing a feeble phosphorus glow, it arced fifty feet into the air and then plopped into the sea. I turned to Stephen and raised an eyebrow, less than impressed, he shrugged. After a slow count of ten the sea in front of us exploded with lurid sparks, colour and noise. Water fireworks—I had never seen them before—are indeed spectacular.

It was a memorable evening and certainly fuelled Stephen's enthusiasm for buying a boat. Even I was coming round to the idea.

Then we set off for home. Still no wind and so once again the tiny motor was asked to do its best. It was suddenly cold. A cotton jumper I had with me just in case was essential but far from enough. We were going against the swell and sitting on duckboard benches that my backside hadn't experienced since school changing rooms. The return journey took three and a half hours.

'Jackie, how about a trip to Malaga tomorrow?'

'No, there's nothing we really need.'

'There are two or three boat showrooms.'

He ducked, I missed and the subject was dropped for a few days. But when he judged that the bruises on my bum had faded sufficiently, we went back to the subject of boats.

Although an architect by training, he is also a very good salesman. Knowing that 'horsepower' sort of words would leave me cold, he painted a lifestyle picture of lazy days moored off the coast, away from the madding August crowds, diving into crystal- clear water and picnicking in isolated coves. When I finally joined the discussions of what sort of boat we might buy, we both knew it was only a matter of time. I was insistent that it had to be something that would not take us over three hours to travel the distance that a car could do in twenty minutes. Duckboard seats were out of the question and it had to have a toilet—it's a girl thing. My final plea, trying to relate to his technical side, was that it had to be Vroom Vroom not Chug Chug.

We bought a boat. It's a Rinker*!?^. Ask Stephen, I don't have a clue. It is basically a floating bar and on the rare occasions that we use it, it is great fun. It has padded leather seats, a loo, and does Vroom Vroom very nicely. To register a boat it has to have a name. We wanted to call it something Spanish. We went through all our music CD's looking for inspiration, and settled on an old Gypsy King's song 'Bamboleo'—meaning, to sway rhythmically.

BACK TO THE PLOT

We were always going to build on the empty plot next to Casa Carolina one day, but during our first three years of retirement, we had moved into Panificadora and changed most of the floors, gutted the kitchen and landscaped the gardens. We had put pools into Casas Rosa and Carolina and built Carmen in Maro up from its ruins. I was begging for the summer off and, much as I liked Paco and his team, I didn't want to see them again, other than socially, for a long, long time.

Stephen had other ideas. This was the architect's dream. Here was his chance to build from scratch, no restrictions apart from the fact that the site was full of mature trees. How could he weave his design to save as many as possible? We had seven tall pines full of cones, six proud green-black cypress thirty feet high and at least a dozen mimosa that each Spring paraded their yellow fluff like Easter chicks.

Back to the 'paper tablecloth' school of architecture.

This was to be our fourth house to go on the rental market. We designed La Quinta over long lunches. When I say 'we' designed, what I mean is that Stephen designed a beautiful house and when I came up with often charming, but usually fanciful and totally impractical ideas he would turn them into a workable reality. Together we got it right.

I did actually get most of that summer off. The architectural drawing package that Stephen bought for the computer kept him out of trouble for weeks before he even produced a working drawing. Then came the process of obtaining quotes, planning permissions and appointing contractors. Meanwhile, we went back to the fun bit, scouring the old building sites, junk yards and skips, finding, for example a front door of old olive wood with a little iron crossed window. It looked like nothing when we bought it for very little, but after a drink of turpentine and several coats of linseed oil it was proud and magnificent.

Much like the UK in the fifties and sixties, most Spanish people are now embracing anything and everything modern. Wooden doors and windows are being replaced by aluminium double glazing, stone sinks are put out with the rubbish and the traditional crafts are being lost and forgotten. Skips outside old houses are now our treasure troves, although it is still possible to persuade many of the local potters and ironmongers to produce their old work. On first meeting, they proudly show us how far they have moved with the times, producing examples of hideous tiles or gates.

When we explain what we are looking for, they seem bemused and often slightly disappointed; however, without exception they are always delighted with the end result. Manolo, the iron man, told us that he took the gates we asked him to make from Stephen's drawings to show his eighty-year old father from whom he had learnt his trade. It made his week.

We had been impressed by Jose, who had built the shells for the pools in both Carmen and Carolina. Since then he had grown his offer to include the concrete structures for houses, essential because we are deemed to be in an earthquake zone. Although the last recorded tremor to do any real damage was in eighteen ninety-nine, we often read in the local papers that there has been enough of a wobble to register, the most recent only a month ago. So Jose got the job of structure, after which the builders would move in.

'Which building team are you going to use?'

'Paco's.'

'Every time you do, you swear it will be the last.'

'And I'm sure this will be no exception.' It wasn't.

In the Spring of the year 2000, the digger arrived to excavate the foundations that had been marked out by walking the site trailing handfuls of sand to define the lines. The skill of the operator was impressive. He used the scoop with the ease of a giant third hand to gouge out the earth. Paco was standing with us watching the first ground breaking; he always seems to be around for the exciting moments but never for the day to day grind that is always part of the building process.

'By the way, Paco, I tried to get you on your mobile number yesterday, but got nothing. Has the number changed?'

'No. I got rid of it. People kept calling me.'

Four open-bed lorries were shuttling the excavated earth away. It was very poor quality soil, not worth keeping. About two feet down the machine began to come up with huge rocks and boulders, Paco began muttering about the extra cost of removing them, as they would have to go to a different place by different lorries. They stayed, and now form the most beautiful rock gardens. Visiting friends tell us that since the craze for garden improvement programmes on British television, the huge lumps of ragged rock flecked with quartz that we would have had to pay to be removed, are now selling for a fortune.

Two habits were established during the building of La Quinta. Almost every evening we would take a bottle of wine and walk the site at around six thirty, just after the builders had left. Every day there was progress, from bare concrete columns to the bricks that began to form walls. We nearly came to blows at this stage because I couldn't believe that some of the rooms were going to be big enough even to swing a cat, but Stephen was confident and used to the false illusions that appear at this stage of building. As it turned out you could easily swing two cats in even the smallest rooms, something I have never actually tried, but have often been tempted.

The roof went on. The two concrete ramps that would eventually become the staircase to the upper floor meant that for the first time I saw the spectacular views down to the sea and up to the mountains from that level.

I hate heights. Standing on a chair is a huge act of bravery for me and therefore I had never been persuaded, despite much hand clapping and shouts of Go Go Go from our builders, to climb the ladder and balance on a concrete girder. Until then, I had had to content myself with listening to Stephen waxing lyrical about the views. Every day there were decisions to be taken; to watch a house grow from a drawing, changing from two dimensions to three was both an education and a delight.

Our other habit was generated by Ron and Anne, an English couple who had lived here for many years and were only five minutes walk away from La Quinta. Stephen met Ron through golf and I was subsequently introduced to Anne at a restaurant in the mountains above the village. A classic example of the attraction of opposites, we all got on famously. Ron was a big loud bear of a man, always the life and soul of the party, telling jokes and buying rounds. Beneath this brash exterior was one of the warmest souls I have ever been lucky enough to meet. He was an OK golfer and a very, very talented squash and tennis player with a penchant for loud silk shirts and prawns pil-pil.

JACKIE TODD

Larger than life would have been a good description
for Ron, and I really hope that is true, because he died
early last year.

The builders always finished at three on Friday afternoons, having worked through their lunch hour. Almost every Friday, Ron and Anne would arrive with a
chilled bottle of wine and smoked salmon sandwiches.
Both of them had a fondness for white trousers and
shoes. The place was filthy and we never knew where
to suggest they sat. They were friends of the kind that
stuck to their standards of dress, but still visited us
anyway. Over time, we progressed from perching our
bums on breeze blocks in the garden, to sitting on the
covered terrace and finally eating our lunch on the
newly installed green granite slab that was the terrace
table. Every week, as Ron watched the house grow, he
became more and more insistent that we should move
into it. It became a joke between us. Ron would argue,
quite rightly, that there would be much more garden
space for our four dogs, and for the ones that we were
bound to acquire in the future. I would counter that
we were never going to have more than four dogs, and
anyway, we had not designed the house for us. My
home and heart were now settled in La Molineta. Having spent a nomadic life I was never going to move
again.

THREE LITTLE SHITS

——————

By the following March, Stephen, Lourdes and I were painting the new house. The builders had finished most of the interior and were laying the terracotta terrace tiles and building planters around the pool. It takes a lot of hours and hard work to paint a house from scratch; the newly plastered walls drink up the first two coats in a most depressing way. A room will look good when you finish of an evening, yet by morning the walls once again seem grey; bare wood doors and window frames behave in the same way. We spent a small fortune on paint, brushes, and white spirit in the village ferreteria, and had the free baseball caps, T shirts and pens all carrying their bright green logo 'Pinturas Andalucia' to prove it. To get the cement off of the tiles requires agua fuerte— literally translated as strong water. This is a bit of an understatement. Agua fuerte is hydrochloric acid, and as you pour it on the tiles the excess cement turns green, bubbles and froths. As we worked backwards across the floors, no matter how careful we were, our hands and legs came up in blisters.

The plot had always been enclosed by three-foot high dry stone walls and wrought- iron gates. One morning Stephen dropped me at the house on his way up to the village for yet more paint. Remembering that we also needed gloss and more masking tape, I ran back to the gate.

'Stephen wait, we need more... Oh shit... Oh shit... OH SHIT!'

By the gate, inside our enclosed land, were the piles of empty wooden pallets that the bricks and tiles had arrived on. From behind these appeared a tiny jet black puppy swiftly followed by another, motley black and brown, and then yet another, again jet black but with classic border collie white markings of face, socks and tail. They stood there, their baby blue eyes wide and staring, huddled together and trembling.

'Stephen, I think you had better come here.'

'Darling are you all right?'

'I'm fine. Well, I was, but look.'

'Oh shit.'

'How did they get here?'

'How do you think? Someone has dropped them over the wall. They haven't parachueted in have they? It's probably someone who knows just how daft we are. Not this time though; we can't have any more dogs.'

'I agree.'

Plans to paint that day were forgotten. Stephen went

home with instructions to return with milk and food. Charly, Domingo, Niña and Tin Tin had long been weaned onto a summer diet of dry biscuits and kitchen scraps with bones as treats, but these little bundles were far too small to manage hard food. Stephen returned with two packets of Jamon Serrano and a carton of milk. They were starving. The all-black puppy was the boldest of the three and was soon wolfing the ham from my hand, whilst I called him a little pig. The other two hesitantly followed his lead. After a breakfast fit for kings, they were much more relaxed and friendly and I checked out their 'bits', establishing that we had two boys and a girl.

The girl, black with white, was the image of the sheepdog puppies in one of my all- time favourite smiley movies about a pig called 'Babe'. Exhausted by their plight and with full bald little pink bellies, they cuddled up together into a corner of the bare dusty floor and were soon fast asleep. One breathing bundle of fur, it was impossible to define where one started and another stopped.

We sat watching the sleeping puppies, slightly stunned. The four dogs we had were with us as the results of our decisions to take on another dog; these three had been dumped upon us.

'Right. Who do we know that wants a dog?'

'Jackie, nobody around here wants a dog. If you want a dog, there are hundreds around here, you know that. Why do you think these have been abandoned.'

'O.K. Who do we know that doesn't yet know that

they want a dog?' I had been in sales and marketing for twenty years.

Whilst I was busy trying to think of potential homes for them, Stephen was busy trying to work out who might have left them here in the first place in order to return them promptly.

Almost our first tenants in Casa Rosa were Lyn and Tony, a couple from Devon that we grew to like very much. They went on to spend many holidays in our little house in Maro and, like us, fell in love with Spain. On their retirement they moved out here, settling in a peaceful spot close to Lake Vinuela with their three springer spaniels. We met regularly for lunch.

'How about Lyn and Tony? '

'They already have three.'

'Well, as of this morning, we have SEVEN. It's worth a try.'

Life-long dog lovers, they eagerly agreed to come and have a look at the new arrivals, but only on the understanding that there was no way that they were in the market for a puppy.

We all sat on the newly constructed terrace, amidst the builder's rubble, watching the three of them at play. After their initial nap, the puppies had woken full of the joys of life, eager for more food and ready to explore. I am always amazed at how resilient young animals are but as a trio they were formidable. The fact that they had been abandoned and, I assumed, snatched from their mother, seemed to have been forgotten. Stephen popped home for supplies for us all, returning with tins of tuna, we were out of ham by then, and bottles of wine. It was a lovely afternoon, tempered only by the problem of what to do with the puppies.

The brindle-coloured boy took to Tony and Lyn in a big way and the affection was obviously mutual. I had already started to call him Stumpy, his tail being far shorter than those of his siblings. But despite my best salesman's patter all afternoon, Lyn and Tony were about to leave and we still had the three pups. I had talked about the new lease of life a puppy would give to their much older Springers, about the fact that, being so young, a new puppy would be no threat to the existing pack. I even used the emotional blackmail of telling Stephen that we would have to consider having them put down if we couldn't find homes for them. Four hours and three bottles of wine later, it hadn't worked. Tony remembered that he had left a book that he had borrowed in his car and went to get it whilst Lyn packed up their things. He returned carrying the book and a deep cardboard box. Inside, was an old blanket. He had a big grin on his face.

'We knew the moment you called that we wouldn't be able to resist, but it's been fun watching you two try so hard all afternoon.'

I didn't know whether to hit him or kiss him, so I did both. They chose Stumpy and, quite rightly, immediately renamed him. Pablo. Almost certainly born in Malaga Province, like the artist before him.

One down, two to go, not bad for the first few hours.

We took the little pig and his sister home for the night. Charly, who four years before had thoroughly enjoyed his status as an only child, rolled his eyes in disgust and chuffed. Niña and Tin Tin feigned indifference. Domingo, on the other hand, made them very welcome. Suddenly he was the fourth tallest dog in the house and seemed to relish his new status.

That Sunday we had an invitation to a birthday party and until this point we had been wondering whether or not to go and how to make our excuses. It would be full of ex- pats and not really our sort of thing, but now it would be a great hunting ground for homes for the puppies. Much to their disgust, we gave them a bath; they fluffed up beautifully and smelt delicious. Carrying one each, we arrived and everyone fell in love with them. They were passed around like cuddly toys and I followed explaining their story and pointing out that they were free to good homes. We lost them for most of the afternoon; this was looking promising. But sadly all of the fifty or so people there had a reason why they could not possible have a dog. We left the party as we arrived, carrying one each.

The following Friday, Ron could hardly contain his delight. As usual we were sitting on the terrace of La Quinta with our smoked salmon sandwiches and glasses of wine. This time though, we had puppies playing at our feet. They were still so tiny that we didn't want to risk leaving them alone all day with the older dogs, who, with the exception of Domingo, to a man (sorry Niña), were less than impressed by their arrival.

'Face it Jackie, you two will have to move here now.'

'Why, Ron?'

'Six dogs.'

'No. We have four dogs. We will find homes for these puppies.'

In my heart I knew that this was probably not true and in the few days that we had had them I was so touched by the way they behaved with one another. It was the first time I had seen puppies of about six weeks still together. They needed less attention than a pup of that age on its' own. They explored their new world with such eager enthusiasm, then, when frightened, tired or hungry, ran to each other for comfort. They slept with their arms around each other and, in an act of penis envy, Babe spent most of her days play- fighting, puppy-bowing and trying to chew Piglet's willy off. Piglet. More polite than calling him a little pig, which he was, and Babe, as in the movie, his pretty little sister. They ran around the building site as if joined at the hip, Piglet's pure black tail and Babe's with a white tip fanning through the air like plumes on the helmets of medieval knights.

'We couldn't possibly split them up now. We will have to find someone who will take them both.'

'We can't find anyone who will take ONE.'

'But Stephen, just look at them together.'

'We don't need more dogs.'

'I know that. Cute aren't they?'

'We don't need more dogs.'

'I know. Aren't they just the most adorable things you have ever seen?'

That evening Stephen worked until the early hours redesigning parts of La Quinta to overcome my objections and explanations as to why we could not possibly move there.

It had been designed and built for people on holiday. But it had also been designed and built with a lot of love and care. We chose tiles, furniture and fittings that we would have wanted for ourselves, but there is a difference between a house for holidays and a permanent home. For a start much less storage, smaller wardrobes, less kitchen space. Overnight he created, on paper, a walk-in pantry off the kitchen and a dressing room off the master bedroom. Now they are two of my favourite rooms. We agreed to turn the third bedroom into our study and build a guest cottage at the bottom of the garden. This has turned out to be one of our best decisions: guests are with us but have their own space and we have ours. It meant an extra month's work for Paco's team and knocking holes in a few already painted walls but on the fourth of July we moved in with our SIX dogs.

LOURDES THE LANDLADY

Over the last few years Lourdes has become much more sophisticated. Of course, all things are relative, but money in her pocket has definitely altered her views and there are friends of ours who accuse us of having corrupted her. However, it is a time of change. We may, in her case, have been the catalyst, but I honestly believe the change was inevitable.

For many generations her family have had a small cortijo in the foothills of the mountains about two miles above the village. There are many such buildings around here, scattered seemingly at random. From a distance it looks as if God threw handfuls of white pebbles at the mountainside. Their cortijo, almost identical to ours, was originally used for storing the tools to work the fields and to take siestas away from the blistering heat of an Andalucian summer afternoon. As time went on, another room was added, then cooking facilities. Originally these places had no electricity and only cold water from a well, as indeed ours still has, but nowadays many have a living-room, kitchen, bathroom and one or two bedrooms. It is common in the height of summer for families lucky enough to have such a place to leave the village at the weekends and spend a couple of nights enjoying the cooler air coming down from the mountains.

Julio, the goatherd, still used their cortijo for his afternoon siesta. It is no more than three hundred yards from the corral, home to his three hundred goats. In summer the smells and the flies are really quite impressive. Two summers ago, Lourdes started asking me about renting out houses for holidays. We had visited Lourdes' cortijo many times. It was difficult to find a diplomatic way to tell her that I didn't think it would qualify as most holiday makers' idea of a Spanish villa, though it was, of course, immaculately clean. An old water-storage tank had been lined with an odd assortment of tiles and made a perfectly serviceable pool and the views were fantastic, but it was and would always be, three hundred yards from three hundred goats and very basic.

I was amazed when, a short time later, Lourdes reported that through a Spanish agent she had signed a rental contract with an English tour operator and that her first clients would arrive at the end of that month. I was amazed, Julio was furious. He was losing his bolt hole and anyway, with them both working, they had, as far as he could see, more than enough money coming in for the three of them; there was no need for it.

The first, and last people to rent the place arrived on a Saturday afternoon. Julio, as usual, was out with his herd. We have often passed him many miles from home, squatting on the side of a mountain, an olive tree for shade, casually throwing stones just in front of straying goats with the accuracy of a professional darts player. That day, returning less than impressed to see a rental car parked outside and foreigners sitting on his terrace, he decided to change the site of his Saturday evening ritual.

Kid is a local delicacy, and Sunday lunch, when family are visiting, demands it. So, every Saturday night he butchers to order. That evening the order was for three. In full view of the new arrivals sipping their gin and tonics, he took three baby goats into the side yard of the corral, slit their throats and hung them up to bleed.

The clients left the following day, still hysterical. It was the last booking that Lourdes ever had.

MARBELLA

Lourdes was not the only local person to be disappointed that summer. With a demand for holiday accommodation that far out-stripped supply, the previous winter, all the tour operators had greedily signed up anything and everything, though many of these properties had problems of one sort or another. A common complaint was access roads. People would arrive, often late at night, driving a strange car on the wrong side of the road and have to negotiate tracks to reach their houses that would make a mountaineer blanch, and if it rained whilst they were out, they often couldn't get back.

By way of compensation for their lack of promised income, the tour operators combined forces to offer the disgruntled owners a free weekend in Marbella. Lourdes was delighted; it would be her second trip away from the village. Julio refused to go. There was a stand-off for a few days and then she casually mentioned a programme she had been watching on television about stress and depression. One of the biggest causes of depression, she pointed out, was not getting out enough. It was something very expensive to treat, sufferers often couldn't work. She hoped she wouldn't get it, but it was always possible. It was agreed that they would go to Marbella for one night on the condition that they leave at six the following morning to be back in time to milk the goats. It would be Julio's first night out of his village in his thirty-nine years, and Lourdes's fourth.

They arrived at the hotel in Marbella in Julio's campo van, several years old, normally used to transport animals and far too big to ever have seen a car wash. The back doors have been held together with a piece of rope for years, the exhaust pipe and the winder for the passenger window are long gone and the window stuck in open mode. Twigs and straw sprout from the two remaining hubcaps and it stinks Not thinking to borrow a suitcase, she packed their overnight things in two supermarket carrier bags. That is how they arrived in Marbella, holiday home to the rich, famous and villanous. Marbella, where Hello magazine shoot so many of their doomed happy couple spreads.

In reception she took over from Julio, having had experience of such things. They were given a room on the twelfth floor and Lourdes headed for the lift.

'What are you doing?'

'Waiting for the lift.'

'I don't trust them. Anyway it's only twelve floors. We will walk.'

Outside their room Julio asked Lourdes for the key. She didn't have it. She walked down the twelve flights to be told that her husband had been given a card, which was the key. She walked back up the twelve floors knowing that he was not going to be happy about this.

'You have the key. It is a card.'

'A card. You mean this?'

'I suppose so, yes. The girl at reception says if you put it into the door it will open.'

'Here the doors open with pieces of plastic? Was it the same in London, no keys?'

'No, in London we had keys.'

It took them ten minutes to get the door open, never waiting for the green light before trying the handle. The room's electricity was also operated on the same principle, and they spent their first hour in semi-darkness until Lourdes once more walked down to reception for an explanation and cheated by catching the lift on the way back. Julio, meanwhile, propped a chair under the handle, wedged a shoe under the door, and muttered about not trusting doors without keys, especially in a foreign village.

That afternoon there was a free coach trip to one of Spain's biggest department stores, El Corte Ingles in Puerto Banus. I had taken Lourdes to the sister store in Malaga the year before, and she had loved it.

'Julio, we must go, and it's free.'

'Why must we go? There are plenty of shops in the village. You are always in the shops.'

'But Julio, this is different. It is all the shops in the village and many many more, all in one place, they have everything.'

'Everything? Then we will go.'

It is true that there are now many shops in the village. The ones selling guide books, postcards and gaudy ceramics leap out from the pavements. Whereas the butchers, bakers and general grocers are mainly hidden behind doors covered by woven curtains and have to be discovered. Inside are three or four chairs where the shoppers sit and are in a hurry if they spend less than an hour buying two eggs and a slice of ham. The talk of the quality of the provisions for the day takes second place to the gossip from the day before. Rather different to El Corte Ingles which could be likened to Selfridges.

'Where first, Julio?'

'Well I would like to see the goat department.'

She was caught. Having claimed the store had everything, she could not satisfy Julio with a visit to the pet shop. He sulked for the rest of the afternoon, refused to be impressed at her mastery of the escalators and used the stairs.

When they had first arrived and eventually got into their room, the free bingo tickets for that evening's game in the hotel were sitting on the dressing table. Yet another bonus for Lourdes; she was used to the bingo played at feria.

Standing in front of loud stalls laden with their cheap stereos and enormous stuffed toy prizes, she would then tear her losing tickets into pieces with disdain and, like her fellow players, scatter them on the floor, making the surrounding area look like a good tapas bar in the late afternoon.

That evening, the prizes were cash. The top prize was more than a month's wages for Lourdes. She was almost totally focused, but glanced round for a second to find Julio staring out of the window, his card in his lap.

'Julio, you must pay attention.'

'I have been paying attention. I got all the numbers more than two minutes ago, this game is really boring.'

Lourdes grabbed his card and as she did so, someone on the other side of the room shouted 'Bingo'. She ran to the caller, explained that her husband had never played the game before and yet his numbers had come up first, but of course, to no avail. The following morning, with a heavy silence between them, they left at five to get back to the goats.

That was Julio's first and I somehow suspect his last night away from his village.

THE GREAT ESCAPE

Everyone who tries to pin a breed to Tin Tin comes up with Lurcher. Even after almost four years with us, Tin Tin still weighs next to nothing and, although he is the tallest of all, I can pick him up with ease. Walking with the dogs in the mountains, when T T' s long legs are at full stride he doubles the pace of the others and frequently jumps over their heads to get where he's going. This agility includes the vertical; he is a four legged pogo stick.

The dry stone walls that surround La Quinta were about three feet high before we moved in. With him in mind, we built them up to five feet, but still he escaped. He is now a social animal, making up for lost time. Having been terrified of people for the first year of his life, he now believes they can do no wrong and wants to meet as many as possible. The problem is that he has no road sense. Not only is he a danger to himself but also to drivers, so we commissioned Manolo, our iron man to make railings to run along the top of the wall. Meanwhile, during the day, we tethered him by his lead to a long length of wire pegged firmly into the ground at both ends. It allowed him to move around, seek sun or shade, but not to escape. At night we shut them all in the house against our usual practise of leaving the terrace doors open and letting them come and go at will; it was far from ideal but was the best we could do. Manolo would take three weeks to make and install the railings and then Tin Tin would be free to run within the garden and be safe. Or so we thought. Friends called to say that their neighbours were worried because they hadn't seen Tin Tin for a few days. We had never met these people, but apparently, during our first month in La Quinta, his month of freedom, every evening T T would arrive at their house, half a mile or so from us, to eat his first supper. They had a stock of dog food for him, he ate, slept on their sofa or their bed for half an hour, had a cuddle and then came home.

With the last section of railings in place, we paid Manolo's bill, decided that Tin Tin must be the most expensive mutt in Andalucia, and took a bottle of Cava into the garden to celebrate both his liberty from the wire and also his captivity. The cork popped, we undid his collar and after a few seconds of confusion he realized that he was no longer restricted. He barked with excitement, circled the very large garden several times and kept returning to us with a waggy tail.

'Look at Charly. He was born old, he's definitely been here before. I wonder who he was. This is perfect. Now they are all safe. The puppies are asleep in the grass and Domingo and Niña are enjoying the sunshine. Umm, Stephen, when did you last see Tin Tin?'

'About ten minutes ago, he was on the bottom wall in the corner, Oh no, he can't have.'

He was gone again. As usual he came back within the hour, yet it took us another month to finally make the garden secure. We had to wire up junctions where the railings met at corners until our skinny Houdini couldn't slip through. Welcome to La Quinta also know as Colditz. Every day we check for tunnels and refuse Tin Tin's request for a motorbike.

CLAUDIA

————

Walking back from a long lazy lunch in the church square with my aunt, uncle, Javier, Rosario and their children, we came upon three old women all dressed in their black widows' weeds, tutting and peering at a bundle in the long grass.

It was the opening scene from Macbeth without the cauldron. Here, traditionally the women wear nothing but black for three years after their mothers die, five years in black for the loss of their father and for ever after if they become widows. It was just before the start of the Easter celebrations and all three had obviously treated themselves to a trip to the hairdresser. The older women, whose naturally jet black hair goes almost pure white with age, favour an enhancing tint that, caught in the right light, gives their heads a slightly eerie, faintly purple sheen.

One of these women was in tears. The bundle in the grass was her cat, no more than two years old with teats full of milk and very close to death. Poison is a problem in this agricultural area, where it is used with the usual Spanish abandon. A cat that is a mouser can be unlucky if its catch has already taken the bait. We had lost our Picasso two years earlier in the same way.

She fumbled in her apron and produced a scrap of fluff the size of a small hamster explaining that it was the only surviving kitten, though at only ten days old, it was now sure to follow the fate of the rest. She laid the kitten beside its mother and walked away. The mother was a beautiful Mediterranen tabby, exactly the type I have always coveted, but she must have had a night of passion with a ginger tom and Auntie Margaret and I found ourselves peering down at one of the results.

Of course, the old lady saw me coming. By now we are very well known in the village and, I am sure, have a reputation for being soft with animals. I know we should have just walked on. In fact Stephen, Richard, Javier and Rosario had done just that. When we caught up with them a few minutes later, there wasn't even a flicker of surprise on Stephen's face when my right boob began to take on a life of its own. I have always tucked the little ones down the front of my tops. It seems to settle them, though it has the opposite effect on Stephen. Claudia, our goddaughter, then four and a half, was delighted with the new addition and in a fit of emotion I named the tiny kitten after her. Stephen looked towards the heavens, rolled his eyes and pointed out in a harsh hissy whisper that there was a very strong possibility that it wouldn't survive—and how was I going to explain that to her namesake? Me and my big mouth; he was right as usual.

But survive she did. Much as I love animals, I have always believed that their place in life is second, if only a very minor second, to most humans. So why was I heating milk for her bottle at five in the morning, still in my dressing gown at ten after the next feed, and talking to friends on the phone—there was no way I could leave the house—about the fact that she had slept for five hours the night before? I smelt of milk, my clothes were covered in it and she often peed all over me. She slept in a shoe box on my bedside table wrapped in a pale baby blue cashmere pashmina. Our vet advised that the four hourly feeds I had last seen with Domingo, were, this time, even more important. 'She is too small to know when she is hungry. Unlike a human baby she will just sleep.' Her shoe box was surrounded by three alarm clocks. Within a week she began to move around and quickly figured out how her front legs worked but couldn't master the back and kept going round in circles. But it wasn't long until she could cross the terrace faster than me, though she still loved being swaddled in her blanket and sucking at her bottle so hard that her little ears waggled with the effort.

Domingo fell in love with her. He followed her everywhere, growling at the others when they got too close; he even bared his teeth at Charly. He washed her face after meals and her bottom after—I'm sure you get the idea.

ES LA VIDA

——————

'Es la vida'—'That's life'—is usually heard here in relation to death. When told that anyone over sixty has died, that's the response—es la vida. Infant mortality was once so high in the village that there are two ways to ask an older woman how many children she has/had because there are almost always two answers. Even now babies are rarely baptized with ceremony before the end of their first year, when their chances of surviving are deemed probable.

A death in the family is a sorrow shared by the village. If you die here before about ten in the morning, you will probably be buried late the same day. The church bells ring the death call and the news spreads rapidly. If it's later in the day, you stay overnight in your house, usually laid out on the dining-table, and all the people of the village visit to pay their respects. Whether friends or enemies in life, all come to say good-bye. The men have it easy, standing outside smoking and chatting; the women sit by the body all night and comfort the bereaved. Neighbours in the surrounding houses leave every light burning throughout the night to ward off bad spirits.

Lourdes arrived early one evening to tell us that Paco's father had just died. Although we had only been on nodding terms with Paco's father, Francisco, that was enough. It was expected that we go to his house. Outside there were at least a hundred people standing around, mainly men, including Paco and his younger brother, the local policeman, Jose Antonio, greeting newcomers and accepting their condolences. Inside it was all women.

Leaving Stephen in the street, I took a big breath and entered the house behind Lourdes, watching closely to copy everything she did. The wooden shutters were closed against the late evening sun, the room lit only by candles. Sitting around one side of the open coffin were the new widow, her daughter and two daughter-in-law. All were dressed in black and holding bibles. We joined the queue to kiss the grieving women and then found a little space in the corner of the very cramped room. Some of the women bent to kiss Francisco's cheek, more simply touched his face or his hand with a lingering look. I find it hard to describe why, but it was not the morbid occasion that I had expected. There were tears, of course, but also smiles and occasionally laughter, especially when someone told the story of him getting so drunk whilst his wife was in labour with Paco that he took one look at the newborn baby and went around the village banging on friends' doors at three in the morning to tell everyone about the arrival of his newborn daughter. Of course, his father missing the obvious is something that Paco still has to live with more than forty years later. After two hours of standing there in silence, Lourdes said it would be respectable for me to leave now. I was instructed to leave quietly without goodbyes. 'Goodbyes to the living are not for this night.' She said she must stay for at least another three hours as Francisco's wife was her mother's second cousin. Close family would be there till dawn and traditionally would not eat or drink from hearing the sad news until after the funeral.

Francisco was buried at five the next evening following a Mass in the church. Again the whole village were there. The Spanish, in death as in life, like to be close together.

Graveyards are multi-story constructions, coffins are slid into spaces almost on top of each other and, whilst the mourners look on, the space is bricked up. Later, it is plastered, a glass front is added, behind which are artificial flowers, ornate crosses and normally a picture of the person, often a favourite possession, too. When the graves are of children, their baby photos and cuddly toys make a heart wrenching sight.

November the first is El Dia de Los Muertos, the day of the dead. Bunches of flowers double in price as everyone buys them to take to the graves, candles are lit and many people spend this day, all day, beside their lost ones.

SPANISH POINTERS

NUMBER SEVEN

When La Quinta was still a building site we would often get a visit from a beautiful big black cat with huge, emerald green eyes. He was flirtatious, friendly and sometimes demanded a share of our sandwiches. We enjoyed his company but didn't really give him much thought. Moving in with our brood, four dogs, two puppies and three cats, caused this animal to undergo a personality transplant. He had been quite happy to share what he obviously considered to be his territory with humans in exchange for scraps, but other animals on his patch were a totally different matter.

Pavarotti embarked on World War Three, though having lost his masculinity under the scalpel of Rafael several years before, he was at a distinct disadvantage. His opponent had a full working set of eggs and the attitude to match. Poor Pavarotti. He would limp back from his campaigns literally to lick his wounds, and he still has a big split in his right ear for his troubles.

After one of these battles he seemed particularly depressed and under the weather, so we took him to see Rafael and Dolores who, much to Pavarotti's disgust, took a blood sample for analysis.

During this time, Pavarotti's little sister was of absolutely no help to him. The day we moved into La Quinta, Pantoja took one look around our new house then walked the half mile back to the Panificadora that same night. She repeated this journey at least two dozen times, and we retraced them all to collect her before we finally got her to settle. Butter on the paws may be dismissed as an old wives' tales but by then I was desperate and it worked for us, or rather for her.

Two days later, Stephen was in town at the vet's to get the results of the blood test that, thankfully, gave Pavarotti the all clear. Feline Aids is rife around here and we had been worried that Attila the Cat might have infected him.

'That's a cute little puppy, Rafael, is he yours?'

'He is cute, isn't he, and very bright too, but sadly he is blind.'

Stephen did a double take. The cute little puppy bouncing around the surgery was, occasionally, bumping into things, but that's what puppies do. When called he came running, wagging his stumpy little tail.

Rafael told his story.

An English couple had brought him in a month before. He was theirs, about six weeks old, with a high fever and very close to death. He had distemper. Distemper kills fifty percent of the adult dogs and eighty percent of the puppies that it infects. Rafael and Dolores had spent long days and nights nursing him back to health and were delighted with their success. His stumpy tail was not docked as such; it had been infected and therefore half of it had had to go. This little mite had really been through hell. It was only when he was recovering and strong enough to undergo a full examination that they checked for all the symptoms and side-effects that distemper can cause. They then realized he had not quite escaped; his optic nerves had been severely damaged. He was blind On learning this, his owners asked that he be put to sleep, a request that Rafael refused. They paid their bill and walked away from him.

'We would love to keep him. He's such a brave little dog, and I suppose that is what we will end up doing if we have to, but we live in a flat and are out all day. It is not really fair. Of course what he really needs is space, people who understand dogs, and other dogs around him. Ideally several dogs, then he can become part of their pack and they will then teach him all the things that no human possibly can.'

I wasn't there, of course, but Stephen has described how Rafael came out with this statement. A lot of words from a man of few, and then just left them hanging there.

'Rafael, may I use your phone?'

When the telephone rang that morning, I was in the middle of promising myself that not only would we never, ever, have another dog, but that we would

some how get rid of all the ones that we already had.
Quite a regular occurrence, this time brought about
by the loss of a brand new, never even worn, pair of
(pale blue, soft, soft leather, kitten heel) slingbacks
to the twins', Babe and Piglet's, still needle-sharp baby
teeth.

'It's me, I'm at the vet's. You're not going to like
this.'

'Pavarotti's got Aids?'

'No. Pavo's fine. His blood test was clear.'

'What then. What won't I like?'

'Rafael has a puppy here ...'

'No. No. No. Not in a million years. No way, I don't
care what you say...'

'It's blind.'

'Blind. Oh Stephen. No. Oh no, we couldn't manage, what about the others? No.'

'Apparently, the others are exactly what he needs, a
pack around him. Look, darling, nobody else is going
to take him are they? What do you think?'

Stephen told Rafael that we would take him for a
few days on the understanding that we could return
him if he didn't get on with the others. Or if we simply
just couldn't cope with his disability.

I shut the dogs in the garden and waited for them
to arrive. Every dog we have taken in has, at first, been
overawed by its new surroundings. We are used to
that and are used to helping them, but I couldn't begin
to imagine what a blind puppy would make of it all.

Stephen carried him in. On the phone I hadn't

asked for a description. If we took in dogs on the basis of their looks, we would have fewer than we do (Sorry Tin Tin). As it turned out he was one of the most beautiful little things I have ever seen. Whilst waiting for them, I had been wondering, and to be honest worrying, what his eyes would be like. Ironically they were huge, limpid chocolate brown pools flecked with amber. Looking from above, he was black and short-haired, but he had a caramel lining and matching slightly raised thumb prints over each eye. His ears belonged to a spaniel, as did the feathers on his back legs. We let him wander around the kitchen for a few minutes but knew from experience that keeping him apart from the others for too long was not the way to go. Charly and Domingo were let in first, the oldest and calmest of the lot. They had seen it all before.

As usual Charly chuffed and sniffed and Domingo, after a brief look, went straight to his basket; nobody takes his basket from him and, as usual, he wanted that established on day one.

Next came Niña and Tin Tin. Niña, always the most jealous, growled softly, sat in a corner and sulked. Tin Tin beamed down from his own planet, wagged his long ratty excuse for a tail in welcome and took the opportunity of our distraction to eat the cat biscuits in the pantry. The puppies, the twins, were no problem. Still at the stage where life was one big adventure, they did the bottom sniffing bit and then ran back outside to play.

I once heard an old great aunt of mine explaining to my young cousin why dogs sniff each other's bottoms. He had been watching her two little shi'tzus greeting her friend's Yorkshire Terrier, and to the embarrassment of all but my aunt, he had pointed it out and asked why they do that. This was her reply;

'Many many years ago, well brought-up dogs used to go to school, just like you do now. Every morning when they arrived for lessons they had to take off their tails and hang them on their pegs. One day there was a big fire at the school and the teacher told all the dogs to hurry, to just grab any tail on the way out of the school and put it on, they would sort it out later. But in fact they never did sort it out, and so now when dogs meet each other they aren't actually sniffing each others bottoms, they are looking for their rightful tails.' A sweet story that might just come in useful some day.

Throughout the introductions, Stephen had sat on the floor with the new arrival between his legs, holding him loosely. Without sight, this puppy's other senses were working overtime. His head was up to allow his twitching nose to catch as many smells as possible. Most of the dogs, in turn, had touched him, sniffing an ear, or nudging his chest. Babe had briefly licked his face. Each contact went through him like an electric shock. Not being able to see it coming must have been terrifying, yet his stumpy little tail was still wagging frantically.

'Stephen he's so brave, he breaks my heart.'

'It's going well so far.'

'What's his name?'

'Stevie. As in Stevie Wonder because he's blind and he's black. Rafael chose it, his owners hadn't named him. That says a lot doesn't it?'

'Well, if he stays, the name goes.'

By the end of the day there was no doubt that he was staying. We live in a mainly open plan space, but that first day, as much as possible, we shut the few doors that there are and let him explore. I crossed my legs and sat on my hands, trying physically to stifle the instinct to run to him every time he headed for a wall. Whenever one of the other dogs approached him, he froze, occasionally producing a small puddle. As in all of the five previous times that we have acquired a new dog, or dogs, plans for the rest of the day were lost. We spoilt the others with treats and made a fuss of the newcomer. Later that same evening, having eaten heartily, he tentatively made his way from the kitchen to the terrace. We were sitting, discussing all the potential problems that we may have to face with life with a blind dog. He bounced towards our voices, off walls and chairs, but he made it. Less than an hour later he repeated the same journey to the terrace without bumping into anything. Stopping every few seconds, he seemed to be thinking, planning his next move with the concentration of a chess champion and eventually he arrived at his chosen destination without a single bump.

'Stephen, he is incredible. It's as if he's got radar.'

It had to be, didn't it? Laughing, Stephen scooped up the little thing and kissed the topof his head.

'Welcome to your new home, Radar.'

LIFE WITH A BLIND DOG

After four years here we didn't have a television. Then we cracked, but only up to a point. We still don't have satellite, choosing to watch only Spanish programmes and therefore continue to improve our command of the language. However, living up to the saying that the difference between men and boys, is the price of their toys, when we decided to move to La Quinta, Stephen bought a Bang & Olufsen flat screen TV. It does everything. Radio, CD, DVD, wall-mounted, it turns through forty-five degrees at the press of a phallic control unit; it is the love of his life. Meanwhile, I am in love with the internet. I can order books, play backgammon with people on the other side of the world and send and receive messages from friends.

The day after we got Radar we looked to the internet to see what we could find out about blind dogs. In 0.16 seconds Google came up with five hundred and seven thousand possible sites, five hundred and six thousand six hundred and eighty were about dogs for the blind. Eventually we found what we were looking for and ordered two books from America about caring for blind dogs.

Radar very quickly learnt the layout of the house. It was only changes of level that threw him, or the hoover suddenly appearing in the middle of the floor. That he would hit head on then yelp with surprise. But within a couple of days he could follow us upstairs, though he couldn't get down again. We would find him standing on the edge of a step no more than six inches high, but totally stuck, dropping a fat baby paw over the side to try and test the drop. 'Step' became a very important word.

'Step, Radar. Step. Step.'

It has become our mantra. It is the instruction that he can move forwards safely, and his trust in us makes me want to cry. Hearing it, he just leaps. Now, we could put Radar on the roof say 'Step', and, bless him, he would.

He did so well that by the time the books arrived they were almost redundant. The only real concern we still had was the danger of the swimming pool. Apparently citrus oil was the answer. Dogs, so both books said, hate the smell of citrus. Sprinkle citrus oil, ideally lemon, around any area that you want the animal to avoid and the problem is solved, they won't go near it. In contrast, they love peppermint and a few drops near their beds and water bowls will encourage them to seek them out. Ironically, in this land of oranges and lemons, we covered half of Andalucia looking for the stuff. The best we could come up with was orange oil.

Triumphant, we returned carrying it into the house along with the bag of lemons that someone had left hanging on the gate. Whilst Stephen was trying to wrestle the top off of the bottle of orange oil, Radar and the others munched their way through the bag of lemons we had left on the kitchen floor. So much for citrus. We havn't even bothered trying peppermint; if they want to go somewhere they do, without the need for encouragement, and Radar follows.

As feared yet expected, Radar had his first swim about a week later. Luckily we were both near the pool at the time and Stephen fished him out in seconds. The next time it happened, a few days later, we were sitting on the terrace, laughing at his trying to chase the twins around the garden. He was having a wonderful time. All our other dogs had realised very early on that there was something different about Radar and, as our vet had predicted, they all watched over him. When, in the middle of a game, they noticed that he was standing in a corner, face to the wall, stumpy tail wagging, playing his solo version of hide-and-seek, any one of them might run over and give him a nudge back in the right direction. On this occasion, it was Piglet who spotted that Radar had cornered himself yet again. Piggy ran to him, nudged him to turn around and then ran back to join the game. Radar, nose high in the air, followed him eagerly.

Unfortunately, to reach the others, Piglet chose the shortcut, over the little mosaic waterfall that trickles down through the rocks and into the pool. He cleared it easily in one bound. Radar didn't. We were out of our chairs and running.

'Jackie, Wait.'

'Wait? WAIT? Have you gone mad?'

'We can't live like this. We have got to see if he can get out on his own.'

He surfaced, spluttering. He had gone in at the deep end and therefore was as far away from the steps as was possible. Stephen had to hold me back. All four paws began working frantically and he made it to one side about half way along the pool. From there he doggy-paddled his way along the edge, not that I was expecting back crawl or butterfly, but he made it. The minute his first paw hit the step he knew that he was safe, you could see it on his face. I ran for a towel and gave Stephen hell for the whole episode, though now I can see that he was right. We had to know. Our dogs have free run of the garden, whether we are in or out, and if Radar hadn't been able to get himself out of the pool, all of that would have had to change.

He's only been in once since then. Months later, Stephen left very early one morning headed for the golf course. I turned over and promised myself another half-hour snooze. A good hour later, I was still totally unconscious when something wet landed on my face. Radar, who had, until that day, never been able to jump onto the bed had made it. By the trail of

JACKIE TODD

water leading from the swimming pool steps, across terraces, through the house, up the stairs and into our bedroom, it was clear that, without any help from us, he had survived another dip.

MYSTERY SOLVED

I had long stopped wondering about who had dumped the three little shits with us. Pablo was thriving with Lyn and Tony, and the twins were good, sweet-natured dogs who had settled in well. Like their elder brothers and sister, they enriched our lives. Stephen would still worry the mystery occasionally, like running a tongue around a sore tooth, but I was sure we would never find out, and by now it didn't really matter anyway.

Saturdays are our busiest days, particularly when we have new arrivals in all four houses, and only four hours to get them clean. In theory, people should leave by ten on the morning of departure, but those with evening flights often linger, whilst the new arrivals should not turn up before two, but often do. This is all very understandable and all very annoying. Between the houses, we have five double and seven single beds. All have to be changed even when there has only been one couple staying in a three bed house.

Some, it seems, like to try out every bedroom and why not? After all they are paying for the privilege.

To achieve this feat of industrial scale domestic cleaning we have six cleaners. Lourdes of course, and her elder sister, Aurora, Charo, Aurora' s sister-in-law, together with Carmensita, Rosa and Miriam. Needless to say, they are all related. They work in pairs and the four eldest each have responsibility for a specific house of which they are fiercely proud. Early on Saturday mornings, in part of the basement of the Panificadora, now called the Cueva de Lourdes, there is always a laundry tug-of-war as they fight for their favourite towels and bed linen.

The Cueva is so called because Lourdes and her elder sister were born there. Thirty- seven years ago Aurora, the mother of Aurora, gave birth to the first of her three daughters in a part of what is now our basement. To celebrate this event, the new father went out and bought the new mother her first pair of proper shoes. Until then she had only ever worn home-made woven esparto grass sandels on her feet. This was our part of the Costa del Sol in the mid-nineteen sixties.

The girls call Saturdays 'Los dias del supermacado', their supermarket days. Anything left in the houses is theirs, and again, it is amazing how people differ. There are times when they are lucky if there is a crust from a loaf and a rotting tomato, though Lourdes' goats are always grateful. Other times, the clients must have gone shopping the day before they left, leaving behind nearly full bottles of whiskey and gin, and enough food to last a week. Not all is well received. The small pot-bellied black jar with the bright yellow lid is always handed to us with a grimace. They have now all tried Marmite once, and only once. Adventurous in the early days, they now ask for information about the various travel-size bottles of lotions and potions left in bathrooms. Lourdes arrived one Monday with very greasy hair, carrying the bottle she had found in Casa Rosa the previous Saturday and announced that she was not very impressed with English shampoo. It was hand cream. Carmensita was equally disgusted by the strength of English skin toner which, it turned out, was nail polish remover. Instructions are not needed for the vast array of pool toys that most of our guests leave behind. By the middle of July all the girls have enough inflatable dolphins, sharks and whales to open their own aquariums.

We are very lucky. Occasionally, when one of the team of cleaners can't make it, between them they organize a stand-in. One Saturday about eight months after we had discovered the three little shits, just for that day, we had a new girl on our team. Puri, short for Purificacion. No more than twenty, she was someone that I vaguely recognized but didn't really know. Lourdes introduced her saying that we certainly knew her father, Sebastian, who was often in Antonio's, which indeed we did.

Just after two, as usual, they all arrived back at La Quinta to be paid The dogs greeted them excitedly.

The new girl burst into tears. Everyone looked surprised.

'It's OK. The dogs are all good, not one of them would hurt you.'

She started sobbing her heart out.

'Lourdes, she's obviously upset by the dogs. Tell her to wait outside and I will give you her wages.'

Carmensita remarked that it was strange that Puri was so upset, her family had always had dogs in the campo, she had grown up surrounded by them.

It wasn't until the following Monday that we got the full story from Lourdes. Between sobs, Puri had explained that her dog, Luna, had had puppies. It wasn't the first litter, in fact it was the third and Puri's father was furious at his daughter's carelessness. I felt like telling him it could have been a lot worse. She was an extremely pretty girl.

When the pups were just under four weeks old, she came home one day to find them gone. Her father claimed that he had found a good home for them, but he refused to say where, and for all those months, she believed that he had killed them. Her tears were of delight, not sadness, that two of the three puppies were alive and well after all. By this time she was all smiles, until Lourdes told her that in fact, not only two, but all three puppies were alive and well, the third, Pablo, was thriving too. Then, loads more tears.

OCHO

——

We have a beautiful big old iron bell with clanger fitted to our wall by the front gates. It is totally redundant. The dogs always let us know if someone is approaching long before anyone reaches that bell. Something started them off one morning in mid-August. I peered through the pantry window to see a typical white campo van driving away. Nothing unusual in that, our drive is often used as a turning point on the narrow road between the village and the coast. For the next hour or so one or another would bark every few minutes and none would settle. This was unusual, in August they do not behave as if they are mad dogs or Englishmen and move around as little as possible in the heat of the mid-day sun. But it wasn't until calm old Charly started to butt his head against my thigh and whimper that I realized something was amiss. I walked towards the front gates and saw that someone had dumped what appeared to be an enormous dusty, dirty, big black rubbish bag in our driveway. As I got closer there was a slight movement. The bin liner was a Cyclops. It slowly lifted its head and looked at me through one weeping eye.

Both Niña and Tin Tin were in a bad way when we took them in but nothing compared to this. It was tied to our gates by a piece of thin wire threaded through the tatty piece of dirty old rope that had obviously served as a collar. We don't need another dog. If there had been an available pile of sand I would have buried my head in it immediately. Instead I did the human equivalent, turned heel and fled inside. For the next twenty minutes I pottered around pretending that it hadn't happened or perhaps I had just imagined it. After all it was only last week that I had put the milk in the oven and the casserole in the fridge. I was definitely beginning to have senior moments. I went to check again. No luck, it was still there. In fact it hadn't moved as much as an inch. Slowly I edged towards the gate and without taking my eyes from the huge lump of dog, I carefully untwisted the wire. Then, against all my natural instincts, I started jumping up and down like a madwoman shouting at it to go away, to go home! I kicked and rattled the gates, picked up a small stone from the path and bounced it inches from his nose. Slowly and painfully it stood up, took one faltering sideways step then its legs folded under it. It was midday, the temperature was in the high thirties and still climbing, though luckily the drive was still partly shaded by our tall cypress trees. The logic in my head was telling me to ignore it. Ignore it and it would go somewhere else to seek food and water. The emotion in my heart was saying 'What the hell are you doing? Get it some water at least—and quickly.'

I manoeuvered a water bowl through the narrow slats of the gate, filled it and sat back to watch the matted mass. It shuffled forwards on its belly and drank the lot, then had seconds and thirds. Good, now it would have the strength to be on its way. Throughout this Tin Tin, our four legged pogo stick was on the high wall above the gates watching with interest. T.T. does not have a nasty bone in his body or thought in his mind. These days he just wants to meet and love as many people and animals as possible and he was whining with the frustration of being separated from a potential new friend.

Stephen called from the golf course full of the joys of life. He had had a good round, in fact his best round for over a year, so there was a distinct possibility that we may have to make more room for yet another hideous trophy in the top of the airing cupboard.

'I'll be home within the hour. Let's go out for dinner tonight. How about somewhere on the beach?'

'Great, but we will have to sort the dog out first.'

'What's happened? Which one now?'

'It's not one of ours. Someone has tied the saddest looking thing you have ever seen to our gate.'

'I'm on my way.'

It was over eight months since we had taken on Radar. Since then we had regularly seen stray dogs on our travels, most distressingly wandering along the hard shoulders, or even worse, the central reservations of motorways. But enough was enough, and as Stephen accelerated and I looked over my shoulder wishing them luck as they disappeared into the distance, I consoled myself with the fact that we had done more than our fair share for the abandoned dogs of the area. Having seven dogs, and no intentions of having any more, 'ocho' - the number eight - had become our generic name for any stray that we saw.

'There was a really pretty ocho on the golf course today, looking thirstly at the water in the lake on the seventeenth.'

'Stephen, there were some gypsy boys in the market this morning. They were trying to sell the tiniest puppies from a cardboard box, far too small to be away from their Mum, the puppies I mean, not the boys. There was almost an ocho. There were four of them, but one in particular looked so weak, I was very tempted.'

I went back to the gate to top up the water bowl and without getting up it attempted a wag of its badly docked tail. Now the sun was overhead, there was no shade in the driveway. Knowing that Stephen was on his way and that this poor thing wasn't able to go anywhere of its own accord, I opened the gate and laid a trail of ham in little pieces towards the porch. Weak as he was, he was starving and had an instinct for survival. Shakily, he followed the trail and collapsed in the shade of the porch. Propped against the wall, sitting beside him, talking quietly and stroking gently, it was the first opportunity for me to really have a good look at him. He didn't have ears. Where they should have been was ragged rimmed thick old scar tissue. The eye that could open was brown and bloodshot. The other was covered in burrs and grass seeds that had matted into a brillo pad; a trickle of yellow pus oozed from the corner. I knew the expression, but until then had never met anything that you could describe as having paws the size of dinner plates. His nails were worn and short, both dew claws were broken and hanging, his pads scarred and blistered. His grey coat was filthy and seemed to be home to half the insect life of Andalucia. After a few minutes he shuffled himself around, put his huge head across my legs, sighed deeply and began to slobber and snore, completely ignoring the hundreds of flies that crawled all over him.

Stephen's mother always buys me what turn out to be my favourite clothes. Things that often I would not choose for myself and sometimes put on grudgingly— then never take off - and that day I was wearing a pair of black Betty Barclay jeans that she had said were 'just me'. They were very just me, but they were swiftly becoming infested with all that this mutt brought with him.

This was how Stephen found us, sitting on the floor of the front porch. He left the car at the edge of the driveway and walked towards us slowly, stopping about six feet away with a wry smile.

'What a state.'

'I can see that and the dog doesn't look too good,

either. We'll take him to Rafael when he opens at five.'
We left him outside in the shade with more food and
water and I went for a very long, very hot shower.

Stephen easily lifted the dog into the car - he showed
no resistance - and then carried him into the surgery.
Dolores, Rafael's wife, was on duty together with Victoria, a young newly qualified vet who had joined
their practice earlier that year. Victoria is extremely
attractive, so much so that since then, if one of the
animals as much as sneezes, Stephen starts muttering
about taking it to the vet just to be on the safe side.
The minute they saw the dog, they both had tears in
their eyes. He stood placidly, swaying slightly whilst
they examined him With a check of his teeth Dolores
said he was about six maybe seven years old, roughly
the same age as Charly. He looked ninety if he was a
day.

'He's badly dehydrated, obviously, he's under-weight
but worse, long-term under-nourished. Until we can
get that eye open I won't know how bad it is, and as
for the state of his coat'… she trailed off.

'What happened to his ears, Dolores?'

'It's common in the campo, although the practice
is dying out now, thank goodness, but at one point
all working dogs had their ears and tails cut as puppies. Though in twenty years I have never seen such
a bad case. This looks as if it was done with a blunt
penknife.'

'Dolores, we are going to have to try and find a
home for him. If you need to shave him in places to

get the worst out, it might be better to do it all over otherwise he will look more moth-eaten that ever.'

'Leave him with us for a couple of hours, we will see what we can do. Come back at eight.'

The working brown eye watched us as we walked away and he sighed deeply as if to say 'I knew that was too good to be true.' From outside I peeked back through the window. He was still watching the door, still swaying. The empty doorway seemed to mark the end of a short chapter in what seemed to have been a very hard life. Yet he stood there, I suppose he had no choice, looking resigned to facing whatever life was going to throw his way next. Although huge, he looked weak, pathetic and so very vulnerable.

We went to a nearby tapas bar, ordered a bottle of wine, chewed absentmindedly through the ham and olives and sat staring into our glasses in silence. My mind was racing. We already had too many dogs. How was I to even begin to explain that I had fallen instant-ly in love with this one? Stephen broke the silence.

'Well, where do we start? The rescue charities, I sup-pose, and there is a chap I play golf with sometimes, Brian, he has a lot of land and has built a special com-pound for all the strays he has taken in. I think he has about a dozen.'

'But they don't live with him, do they? In the house I mean. They don't lie by the fire at night, get told off for jumping on the bed, or get to smell what's cooking in the kitchen, have passing cuddles, treats, pats and strokes all day.'

'Well no, they don't, but he would have a much better life than he has obviously been used to.'

'Stephen... I think you would have to agree that you are totally responsible for the fact that we now have seven dogs, wouldn't you?'

'Yes, I suppose so.'

'Well it's my turn now. I want to keep him, I really, really want to keep him.'

As usual my timing was lousy. He had a mouthful of wine. He inhaled and almost choked.

'He is the size of a small horse.'

'Yes.'

'He's probably never been inside a house and won't be house trained. Can you imagine the size of the....'

'Probably. And, Yes I can.'

'You heard what Dolores said, he may only have the use of one eye.'

'That's one more than Radar.'

'He might be a cat killer."

'True.' Now that would be a problem.

'We don't need another dog.'

'That is also most certainly true. Look, he's a big dog and therefore, at six or seven, half-way through his life, a life that doesn't appear to have treated him too well so far. We could change all that. I know it doesn't make sense. I can't explain it. There is just something so sad yet so gentle and brave about him, but something more than that. I feel. I feel. I can't explain it, and I know it sounds crazy, but I feel that I KNOW him. I really want us to keep him. Please.'

'O.K.'

'And another thing, I think that he ... did you say O.K.?'

'Yes, I said O.K. So come on, it's nearly eight, how appropriate, let's go and see how Ocho is doing.'

Many years ago someone told me 'When you have sold, stop selling.' I didn't say another word.

Back at the vet's there was a shiny black dog sitting under the grooming table with the hot air blower ruffling it's coat. Dolores was at her desk doing paperwork but there was no sign of Ocho, she smiled as we walked in.

'Doesn't he look better? It took the two of us two hours with the curry comb and a whole big bottle of shampoo, but he was so good, he didn't complain once, though we must have hurt him at times I have rarely met such a sweet-natured creature.'

Confused, we looked under the table again, it couldn't be—but it was. Ocho wasn't grey, he was jet black with a white blaze down his chest and white front paws. His bad eye was now open and clear. Hearing our voices, he had stood up and was wagging what was left of his tail. We let him out of the canine hairdryer and he immediately came and sat quietly at our feet. I looked down and our eye contact was electric.

'Finding a home for him won't be easy. I will put a notice on our pinboard, and ask around, but most people want younger and certainly smaller dogs. One of the animal rescue charities may have a kennel space, though I doubt it.'

'We have decided to keep him.'

She burst out laughing. 'I just don't believe you two, but I couldn't be more happy. He is a very lucky old boy.' We chose a collar and asked about vitamin tablets, which Dolores agreed would give him a much-needed boost.

'What do we owe you, Dolores?'

'Twelve Euros. Seven for the collar and five for the vitamins.'

'And for the rest?'

'That was only time and if you are prepared to give yours and your love, we will gladly give ours. There is no price on saving an animal's life and giving it a loving home.'

This was not the first time we had encountered their kindness and generosity towards animals. About three years ago, before the motorway link from Malaga was completed, the coast road took all the traffic and was very busy. We were filling up the car in a garage on the outskirts of Nerja when there was the most dreadful scream that seemed to freeze time. The garage forecourt was busy and everyone turned, seemingly in slow motion, in the direction of the noise. Then Stephen and another man were running, dodging the traffic and bending by something in the grass on the far side of the road. Even now when I remember that scream I get goose pimples, it had sounded human. Seconds later Stephen was back.

'Get in quickly, we need Rafael.'

Stephen double parked outside, I ran in. There were three or four people with assorted animals in the waiting-room and the door to the surgery was open.

'Rafael, a dog's been hit on the main road. Can you help?'

Without a word he grabbed his Gladstone bag and was in the car in seconds. It could not have been more than five minutes since the accident that Rafael was kneeling at the dog's side, but we were too late; the pretty young pointer was dead. We drove Rafael back to his surgery at a more sedate pace and asked to pay for his time. He refused any payment, saying that it was just a shame he couldn't have helped.

We took Ocho home. The minute we opened the back door of the Land Rover he jumped in without help. Despite still being very weak, he was determinedly going wherever we were, and the fact that he was now clean, less dehydrated and could see out of both eyes had obviously given him slightly more energy and confidence.

We knew that introducing this new member to our pack was going to be our biggest challenge so far. Not only was Ocho the same age and larger than Charly, he was also an un-neutered male; two sets of doggie balls in the same house had great potential for problems. Luckily, too weak to show any signs of aggression, he flopped in a corner and let the others sniff and investigate. Charly looked less than impressed but that was normal.

It was only after a couple of weeks that the tensions rose. Ocho was getting stronger and more confident by the day, although we had never heard him make a single sound and were beginning to wonder if we now had a mute dog to go with the blind one. He certainly wasn't deaf. He learnt his new name within days and would come, sit and lie down when instructed, but, of course, only in Spanish, so we got used to giving instructions in two languages. Combined with the hand signals that we always use to accompany each instruction, it wasn't long before we had eight bi-lingual dogs. He had obviously, as Stephen predicted, not been inside a house before. He tiptoed around the rugs on the floor as if they were land mines and sat watching television for hours. But not once did he poo or pee inside. This was a contrast to his approach to the garden, which was to bulldoze through and mark everything. Then the growling started. Whenever the two big ones came near each other, which in general they both tried to avoid, there would be much growling and baring of teeth.

The first time they fought I was terrified. We were all in the garden and I didn't see what started it, but never having seen two big dogs have a go at each other before I really believed they were going to kill one another. Luckily they were quite near to Stephen who was watering pots at the time and the hose pipe on full blast quickly split them up.

Three similar incidents and our minds were made up, one set had to go. Working on the principal of 'last in first off,' we booked Ocho an appointment with Rafael. It has worked; although not yet firm friends, they now rub along together quite happily and the others, who had never had a problem from day one, adore him.

Claudia, who I am sure has grown up believing that she is a dog, uses him as a mobile walkway. She jumps onto his broad back and sits with her paws tucked around his neck until he reaches her chosen destination and then goes her own way. This is her third change of affection; after accepting Domingo's initial nannying, her attention moved to Radar. They began sleeping together and we expected them to announce their engagement any day. I thought the delay was due to the choice of ring, she is definitely a big diamond sort of girl. Radar lovingly endured her swinging from his ears and clawing at his tail, I think it was when she started to climb trees that the relationship began to cool. One minute she was there, the next she was gone and no amount of sniffing could find her. A difficult concept for a blind dog. Meanwhile, Pavarotti and Pantoja treated Ocho with the tolerance and slight disdain they reserve for the rest of their canine family.

DON'T EVEN THINK ABOUT IT

Of course, it was stupid to even think about it, let alone allow, even encourage it to happen. But Claudia grew into such an affectionate adorable cat that we couldn't resist. Most afternoons, before siesta, we stroll around the garden and inspect the progress of the plants. Things grow so quickly here that there are literally day-to-day changes. A bamboo, no more than knee high two years ago, is now touching twenty feet. Sapling lemon trees and the grapefruit bush are in fruit, we grow our own delicious stumpy bananas and jasmine invades the terrace. To the left of the drive, where we have no irrigation system, we have planted what has turned into a spectacular cactus bed. Until moving here I had never been a cactus fan, my mother always had three or four in pots on kitchen windowsills that I swear did not grow, flower or change in fifteen years, she used to dust them. To me, until now, they had always been the living dead of the plant world.

The dogs have always joined us on our wanders; we Pied Piper our way around. Ocho picked up the habit very quickly, possibly encouraged by the pockets full of dog treats that we always carry. He has turned into a foodie. The six or seven years of his famine have resulted in a dog that can't say No. To begin with he needed fattening up but now he needs to enroll in Weight Watchers. Ocho has become Ochissimo. Javier recently described him as the 4 X 4 of the dog world. He has also remembered, or more probably learnt for the first time, how to play, how to bark and how to just have fun. Number eight, these days, is a small shaggy Shetland pony masquerading as a dog. He loves life and hates the flies that he used to ignore; in fact, now, he has the energy to take flies as a personal insult.

Claudia always accompanies us on our vueltas, demanding her fair share of the treats. We were half-way round the garden late one afternoon when I casually mentioned that it would be wonderful if she had kittens. We had already discussed that the time was near to take her to Rafael for her operation, and I expected Stephen to dismiss my romantic musings in a flash. But, he did it again.

'Yes. Why not?'

I didn't say another word. Time went on and a trip to the vet for Claudia was not mentioned again.

Soon after Claudia's first birthday, I was hanging out the washing when a gigantic ginger cat appeared. It rubbed around my legs and refused to be frightened away. Two hours later, it had been joined by a rather fetching tabby and our neighbour's jet black cat from hell. By the following morning, a small black and white moggie with a scabby, runny nose and a sore paw had added its number to the throng. They all had one thing in common—huevos. At last the penny dropped. Claudia was ready for her suitors.

Back in the house, I took my maternal responsibilities seriously. I sat little Claudia on my lap and explained the facts of life. I agreed with her that it was a touch disappointing that between all four of them there was not a guitar, a bunch of flowers or even a box of chocolates in sight. I promised that whoever she chose, we would respect her decision and love them like our own, but urged her to give serious thought to the tabby. She jumped off my lap, stretched lazily with the flexibility of an Olympic gymnast, and walked away. Forty-eight nail biting hours later she was back, refusing to answer a single question.

Was she or wasn't she? A Google search gave me facts, but not the information I was looking for. Only Claudia could do that. Gestation for cats is normally between fifty-eight and sixty-four days, it said. First time mothers usually have two to four kittens, it said. OK, if she was pregnant we were looking at the very end of April or the first week in May and she would probably, if conforming to the average, have three babies.

She couldn't possibly be pregnant. She was climbing trees as usual, eating as normal, playing rough and tumble with the pack and showing no signs of cravings for charcoal, bitter chocolate or pickled onions. She hadn't even put on weight and then, suddenly, almost overnight, she blossomed. Her skinny little frame remained just that, but she developed a low slung bum bag and although I wouldn't have thought it possible, she became more affectionate than ever.

Back to the internet. 'Cats rarely have their kittens where you would expect or want them to. Many leave home to have their litter, especially if they perceive a threat to the offspring.' Well no problem there, no threat here, Claudia thought I was her mother and all eight dogs loved her as much as she loved them. Eight dogs. Would she suddenly perceive that as a threat? I became obsessed with the idea that she would go away to have the kittens and then die in the process.

By the beginning of May I was jumping every time she made a sound, whereas Claudia seemed to be on valium. She was following her usual routine, only at a slightly slower pace and with a big smile on her face. Our house, normally rather minimalist in style, looked like the depot of a famine relief charity. I had put old rugs, jumpers and blankets in every possible corner, shelf and wardrobe. In the spare bathroom there were piles of fluffy towels, sterilized water, dental floss and newly sharpened nail scissors. Dental floss was apparently the perfect thread to tie the umbilical cord if the mother was not able to bite through it herself.

I now knew about such things. I had surfed for hours learning to be the perfect midwife to our feline friend and almost frightened myself to death in the process, reading of all the potential dangers and the horror stories. Stephen had every confidence in her, saying that I was overreacting as usual, and that for Claudia, a typical campo moggie, it would be like shelling peas. As a mother, it was an expression that I hated.

'When is the next full moon?'

'I don't have a clue. Why do you ask?'

'I've just been speaking to Javier. He says that Clouds will have her kittens on the day of the full moon.'

Locally, the moon's activities carry great weight. Crops are planted when it is waxing and, months later, harvested only as it wanes. Many years before, Lourdes had been appalled that I was going to have my hair cut during a waxing moon.

'Jackie, por favor. You are wasting your money, your hair will grow again so quickly, wait two weeks.' She also, advised that I should wax my legs when the moon was waning—nothing was growing—it would last much longer.

I guess every country has its old wives' tales.

MAY 4TH 2004

Our study, lined with books and photographs, painted a pale Andalucian blue, is our animals' official bedroom. There are eight wicker baskets with plump cushions hugging the walls, and, with the exception of Domingo (My basket is my basket, the one in the corner, green cushion and away from the door. Mine. OK?) they all seem to pick and choose at random. It works well during the day, and for all of five minutes after we have gone to bed. Then they begin to creep up the stairs. Niña is always first, she favors the bath mat, then Tin Tin heads for the shower. Babe and Piglet drop to their bellies, shuffle under our bed and still sleep entwined. Radar wanders around until he corners himself and sleeps where he drops. Ocho, the protector, settles at the top of the stairs and competes with Stephen to see who can snore the loudest. Only Charly and Domingo, our first two, and the best trained, stay in the study in their baskets overnight.

Stephen bought Claudia a foam igloo cat bed when she was no more than three months old. We made a space for it, under the computer, between a couple of the wicker baskets. I didn't think that she would ever use it, in my experience, cats always sleep where they want to. She loved it from day one.

Early evening on the fourth of May, I was checking our e-mails when she strolled into the study, gave an even louder than usual purr, rubbed herself against my leg, and climbed into her igloo. The first kitten arrived within minutes. It was Charly who alerted me. He came to stand beside me and shoved his nose inside Claudia's tent. He reversed rapidly, he sneezed, chuffed and lay down only inches away, his tail wagging like crazy. I watched fascinated as she rolled onto one side, lifted a back leg and allowed a tiny, slimy sack, about the length of my little finger, to slip into our world. Immediately she stood and began to lick it, but within seconds she lay down again and produced another. I was ready for this. 'If the newborns arrive in quick succession, the new mother may not be able to cope. It is essential that the umbilical sack is removed quickly or the kitten may suffocate. Gently wipe the sack away with a sterilized towel dipped in pure water.'

It took me less than a minute to run to the bathroom, collect my emergency kit, and be back at Claudia's side, but, I was too late. Charly had beaten me to it. With his head inside the igloo, he was as intent as the new mum, licking blood smeared mucus from the second kitten. Claudia settled down with her new babies and Charly went outside for some air. On his way he had obviously told the others of the news. He looked so proud that I kicked myself for not having bought him some cigars to hand out. Two by two, as dictated by Noah, the dogs came to visit. They all stuck their noses into the 'crib' and gently licked the kittens whilst little Claudia purred like a lioness and smiled contentedly.

The drama, or rather the lack of it was over. Claudia had pushed the two newborns towards her teats and they were suckling happily. Just over an hour later, I had almost finished sending the news around the world to all our animal-loving friends when, with equal lack of fuss or fanfare, Number Three arrived. This time, Claudia had five or six minutes to clean and welcome it before the fourth and the smallest of the lot made her debut.

We sat on the terrace late that night celebrating the arrival of four perfect kittens and watching that night's full moon shining down on us. For Claudia, still smiling though asleep with her kittens, it did seem to have been rather like shelling peas.

As we suspected, she has turned out to be an excellent mother. Her first born, a boy, was followed by three girls. Growing up surrounded by dogs since she was ten days old, she has passed her acceptance to her kittens who within three weeks, were more or less mobile and totally fearless. This time it is Babe who has become second Mum to the new arrivals.

The first time one of the babies fell two steps down the terrace stairs, she was there within seconds and, gently picking it up by the scruff of its neck, carried it back to Claudia. Rafael approved. He pointed out that Claudia had produced exactly what the continuation of the species demanded, three child-bearing females and a strong healthy first-born male to sire them. I bit my tongue hard and smiled. In memory of my father, first-born boy followed by six sisters - so I guess my grandmother did even better in that respect - we have called him William and the name seems to sit comfortably with him. The youngest two of Claudia's girls, Luna and Paloma, are now happily installed in their new home with Javier, Rosario and our god children. William and his sister Paintbox—already shortened to PB - who has a little bit of every colour possible—are staying with us. Claudia still refuses to name the father. Perhaps she is planning to write her own book one day, although she knows I disapprove of kiss and tell.

So, eight years, six houses, eight dogs and five cats. Still no Spanish Pointer. But with William, Claudia has fulfilled yet another of our dreams. He is the most beautiful and perfect Mediterranean Tabby, complete with the charcoal stripes that match across his front legs and the Cleopatra eyeliner.

ISBN 141206490-2